MEDIA VIOLENCE

OPPOSING VIEWPOINTS®

Louise I. Gerdes, *Book Editor*

Daniel Leone, *President*
Bonnie Szumski, *Publisher*
Scott Barbour, *Managing Editor*
Helen Cothran, *Senior Editor*

OPPOSING
VIEWPOINTS®
SERIES

GREENHAVEN
PRESS®

THOMSON
———— ✶ ————™
GALE

San Diego • Detroit • New York • San Francisco • Cleveland
New Haven, Conn. • Waterville, Maine • London • Munich

THOMSON

---★---

™

GALE

© 2004 by Greenhaven Press. Greenhaven Press is an imprint of The Gale Group, Inc., a division of Thomson Learning, Inc.

Greenhaven® and Thomson Learning™ are trademarks used herein under license.

For more information, contact
Greenhaven Press
27500 Drake Rd.
Farmington Hills, MI 48331-3535
Or you can visit our Internet site at http://www.gale.com

LIBRARY OF CONGRESS CATALOGING-IN-PUBLICATION DATA

Media violence / Louise I. Gerdes, book editor.
    p. cm. — (Opposing viewpoints series)
    Includes bibliographical references and index.
    ISBN 0-7377-2012-3 (pbk. : alk. paper) — ISBN 0-7377-2011-5 (lib. : alk. paper)
        1. Violence in mass media. 2. Mass media and youth. I. Gerdes, Louise I.
    II. Opposing viewpoints series (Unnumbered)
    P96.V5M428 2004
    303.6—dc21   2003044810

Printed in the United States of America

> "Congress shall make no law...abridging the freedom of speech, or of the press."

First Amendment to the U.S. Constitution

The basic foundation of our democracy is the First Amendment guarantee of freedom of expression. The Opposing Viewpoints Series is dedicated to the concept of this basic freedom and the idea that it is more important to practice it than to enshrine it.

Contents

Why Consider Opposing Viewpoints?

"The only way in which a human being can make some approach to knowing the whole of a subject is by hearing what can be said about it by persons of every variety of opinion and studying all modes in which it can be looked at by every character of mind. No wise man ever acquired his wisdom in any mode but this."

John Stuart Mill

In our media-intensive culture it is not difficult to find differing opinions. Thousands of newspapers and magazines and dozens of radio and television talk shows resound with differing points of view. The difficulty lies in deciding which opinion to agree with and which "experts" seem the most credible. The more inundated we become with differing opinions and claims, the more essential it is to hone critical reading and thinking skills to evaluate these ideas. Opposing Viewpoints books address this problem directly by presenting stimulating debates that can be used to enhance and teach these skills. The varied opinions contained in each book examine many different aspects of a single issue. While examining these conveniently edited opposing views, readers can develop critical thinking skills such as the ability to compare and contrast authors' credibility, facts, argumentation styles, use of persuasive techniques, and other stylistic tools. In short, the Opposing Viewpoints Series is an ideal way to attain the higher-level thinking and reading skills so essential in a culture of diverse and contradictory opinions.

In addition to providing a tool for critical thinking, Opposing Viewpoints books challenge readers to question their own strongly held opinions and assumptions. Most people form their opinions on the basis of upbringing, peer pressure, and personal, cultural, or professional bias. By reading carefully balanced opposing views, readers must directly confront new ideas as well as the opinions of those with whom they disagree. This is not to simplistically argue that everyone who reads opposing views will—or should—change his or her opinion. Instead, the series enhances readers' understanding of their own views by encouraging confrontation with opposing ideas. Careful examination of others' views can lead to the readers' understanding of the logical inconsistencies in their own opinions, perspective on why they hold an opinion, and the consideration of the possibility that their opinion requires further evaluation.

Evaluating Other Opinions

To ensure that this type of examination occurs, Opposing Viewpoints books present all types of opinions. Prominent spokespeople on different sides of each issue as well as well-known professionals from many disciplines challenge the reader. An additional goal of the series is to provide a forum for other, less known, or even unpopular viewpoints. The opinion of an ordinary person who has had to make the decision to cut off life support from a terminally ill relative, for example, may be just as valuable and provide just as much insight as a medical ethicist's professional opinion. The editors have two additional purposes in including these less known views. One, the editors encourage readers to respect others' opinions—even when not enhanced by professional credibility. It is only by reading or listening to and objectively evaluating others' ideas that one can determine whether they are worthy of consideration. Two, the inclusion of such viewpoints encourages the important critical thinking skill of objectively evaluating an author's credentials and bias. This evaluation will illuminate an author's reasons for taking a particular stance on an issue and will aid in readers' evaluation of the author's ideas.

It is our hope that these books will give readers a deeper understanding of the issues debated and an appreciation of the complexity of even seemingly simple issues when good and honest people disagree. This awareness is particularly important in a democratic society such as ours in which people enter into public debate to determine the common good. Those with whom one disagrees should not be regarded as enemies but rather as people whose views deserve careful examination and may shed light on one's own.

Thomas Jefferson once said that "difference of opinion leads to inquiry, and inquiry to truth." Jefferson, a broadly educated man, argued that "if a nation expects to be ignorant and free . . . it expects what never was and never will be." As individuals and as a nation, it is imperative that we consider the opinions of others and examine them with skill and discernment. The Opposing Viewpoints Series is intended to help readers achieve this goal.

David L. Bender and Bruno Leone,
Founders

Greenhaven Press anthologies primarily consist of previously published material taken from a variety of sources, including periodicals, books, scholarly journals, newspapers, government documents, and position papers from private and public organizations. These original sources are often edited for length and to ensure their accessibility for a young adult audience. The anthology editors also change the original titles of these works in order to clearly present the main thesis of each viewpoint and to explicitly indicate the opinion presented in the viewpoint. These alterations are made in consideration of both the reading and comprehension levels of a young adult audience. Every effort is made to ensure that Greenhaven Press accurately reflects the original intent of the authors included in this anthology.

Introduction

"For over a century, the issue of violence in the media has been a prominent area of concern for government officials, academics and the general public. Research has been conducted and conferences convened, but the issue remains as contentious as ever."

—University of California at Los Angeles
TV Violence Monitoring Project

Popular culture has historically been the subject of scorn, especially its more violent forms. In 1751 author Henry Fielding chided eighteenth-century English culture for the "too frequent and expensive Diversions among the lower kind of People." Fielding censured pastimes such as bear baiting, which involved the pitting of bears, sometimes blinded, against other animals, particularly dogs. The impact of popular culture on youth has been of particular concern. Early in the nineteenth century, novelist George Meredith complained that the Punch and Judy puppet show, in which Punch and his wife Judy physically abuse each other, "inspires our street-urchins to instant recourse to their fists in a dispute." Nineteenth-century detractors also warned of the dangers of reporting on crime and vice in newspapers, claiming it would lead juveniles to imitate lawless and immoral behavior.

Media analysts note that critics most often direct their attacks against the most recent entertainment medium as it becomes more popular and available to large numbers of people. In his book *Evil Influences: Crusades Against the Mass Media*, psychologist Steven Starker writes, "Each technological innovation, or new media application, promptly has been declared a serious threat to the character and mental abilities of children, the behavior of teenagers, the morality and intelligence of adults, and the sanctity of the American way of life." Fears about the impact of violence in new media have raised particular concern. The pattern of society's response is relatively consistent: Once someone sounds the alarm, the public looks to science for answers and to the government for solutions.

This pattern can be clearly seen in the furor over program content when radio became popular. Media detractors condemned radio for airing "popular" music, believed to inspire sinful behavior, but it was radio's early developer, Lee de Forest, who expressed concern about the effects of broadcasting crime dramas. He bemoaned the state of radio in a 1950 speech: "What have you gentlemen done with my child? He was conceived as a potent instrumentality for culture, fine music, the uplifting of America's mass intelligence. You have debased this child, you have sent him out in the streets in rags of ragtime, tatters of jive and boogie woogie, to collect money from all and sundry, for hubba bubba and audio jitterbug. . . . Murder mysteries rule the waves by night and children are rendered psychopathic by your bedtime stories."

The pattern of society's response to new media was also repeated in the uproar created by the emergence of popular films. Criticism of violence in motion pictures began almost from the new medium's inception. Columbia University psychology professor A.T. Poffenberger wrote in 1921 that movies "might easily become a training school for anti-Americanism, immorality, and disregard for the law." When constituents expressed concern, government leaders threatened the movie industry. In 1934 the federal government pressured the Motion Picture Producers and Distributors of America, under Will H. Hays, to implement a self-regulatory code of ethics. Among the general principles of the code was the requirement that "no picture shall be produced which will lower the standards of those who see it. Hence the sympathy of the audience should never be thrown to the side of crime, wrongdoing, evil or sin." The Hays Code established production guidelines prohibiting movies that inspired criminals or made criminals seem heroic or sympathetic.

The comic book industry was another new media to come under attack. In 1954 psychiatrist Frederic Wertham reported in *Seduction of the Innocent* that "the average parent has no idea that every imaginable crime is described in detail in comic books. . . . If one were to set out to show children how to steal, rob, lie, cheat, assault, and break into homes, no better method could be devised." Wertham alleged that there was a correlation between crime-comics and juvenile delinquency. His work was widely quoted in newspaper and magazine articles. Parents, educators, and concerned citizens were especially upset about the violent messages that crime and horror comics might convey to children and teenagers and began pressuring government to act. In the spring of 1954, a special senate subcommittee, chaired by Senator Estes Kefauver, held hearings on the topic of comic books and juvenile delinquency. The subcommittee report concluded that many of Wertham's claims were exaggerated or unfounded, with no research studies to support them. Nevertheless, the report was critical of the content of crime and horror comics and recommended industry self-regulation. In response, the comic book industry formed the Comics Magazine Association of America and adopted the first Comics Code Authority to promote "good taste and decency."

The same subcommittee that chastised the comic book industry also looked at the relationship between juvenile delinquency and television, and in the years since, hearings on the effects of television violence on children have been common. Of all the media, television has received the most scrutiny. More research has been conducted on television violence than on any other form of media violence. Based on research conducted by William Schramm, Jack Lyle, and Edwin Parker, in 1961 the Schramm Report concluded that although some television was harmful for some children, for most children television was harmless. Public criticism of television violence continued, however, and in the years since the report, thousands of studies have been conducted on television violence. While some analysts continue to claim that the research is inconclusive, government agencies such as the National Institute of Mental Health and the Surgeon General's office have concluded that research does in fact link television violence and real-world aggression. Public concern over the impact of television violence has led to government restrictions. The 1996 Telecommunications Act required broadcasters to develop a ratings system to be used in conjunction with a V-chip, which the Act required manufacturers to install in televisions by 1999. The V-chip allows parents to control access to programs rated too violent for children.

Fears about media violence continue into the new millennium. Authors in *Opposing Viewpoints: Media Violence* examine the controversies surrounding the issue of media violence in the following chapters: Is Violence in the Media a Serious Problem? Should the Government Restrict Media Violence? How Should Society Respond to Media Violence? The authors featured express diverse views on the impact of media violence and how society should respond to it.

Is Violence in the Media a Serious Problem?

Chapter Preface

To answer the question of whether media violence is a serious problem, analysts often cite research conducted on the issue. Those who claim media violence is a serious problem cite studies that establish a link between media violence and real-life violence. Opponents of this link often point out problems with the methods of this research or its conclusions. However, several studies, rarely cited, actually show that media violence has positive effects.

Seymour Feshbach, for example, controlled the television viewing of four hundred adolescent boys in private boarding schools. Over a period of six weeks, half the boys were limited to violent programs, the other half to nonaggressive programs. Before and after controlled viewing, trained observers judged aggression levels. The results revealed that for boys from relatively low socioeconomic backgrounds, aggressive television content seemed to reduce or control aggression. Interpreting this finding, Feshbach concluded that "television fantasies supplement a person's own imagination, and help him discharge pent-up aggression in the same way that dreams and other products of the imagination can do."

In his book *Why Viewers Watch*, Jib Fowles explains that television has proven to calm aggressive impulses in troubled individuals. Fowles argues that "for the segment of the population that has been crushed by the real world, and has had to be removed from it, television is clearly a boon. Anyone who has visited an institution where humans are confined knows that television exerts a calming, beneficent influence." According to Fowles, hospitals, prisons, and asylums use television to calm those who are highly volatile and stimulate those who are depressed.

Another media scholar, Steven F. Messner, examined crime rates among populations with high levels of exposure to television violence. Using Nielson ratings from large metropolitan areas, Messner estimated the audience size of programs rated high in violent content by the National Coalition on Television Violence, an advocacy group that opposes media violence. He then examined the FBI crime rate data for violent crimes in these same communities, including criminal homicide, forcible rape, robbery, and aggravated assault. "The results," Messner explained, "were quite surprising. . . . For each measure of violent crime, the estimate for the level of exposure to television violence is negative." Communities where a large number of people watched violent television programs tended to have low violent crime rates.

Gerhardt Wiebe, former dean of Boston University's School of Public Communications, hypothesized that the entertainment media relieves the stress of socialization for adolescents who must change from rebellious teenagers into productive and therefore conforming adults. Wiebe claims that along with directive and maintenance messages, which support traditional beliefs, the media sends "restorative" messages, which Wiebe claims allow viewers to restore themselves "from the strain of adapting, the weariness of conforming." Analysts such as Richard Rhodes argue that the popularity of music such as heavy metal and rap, violent movies such as *Natural Born Killers* or *Pulp Fiction*, and violent video games and television programs support Wiebe's theory. "Media performances serve vicariously to intensify and then resolve tension, carrying away in the process all sorts of psychic detritus. They make it possible to put on a hero's armor, slay dragons, and then hang up your armor and be yourself. . . . At their most basic, entertainment media take the psychic garbage out," Rhodes claims. To become violent, people must experience real violence, Rhodes maintains.

The nature and extent of the influence of media violence remains the subject of debate, and the authors of the viewpoints in the following chapter examine whether its influence is a serious problem for society.

"With respect to television and movies, existing research already demonstrates a solid link between media violence and the violent actions of our youth."

Media Violence Leads to Youth Violence

Senate Committee on the Judiciary

Violent juvenile crime is on the rise, maintains the Senate Committee on the Judiciary in the following excerpt from their report *Children, Violence, and the Media: A Report for Parents and Policy Makers*. A principal cause of this rise, the committee argues, is the violence that permeates the media. According to the committee, existing research irrefutably links media violence to youth violence. Since Americans know that media violence is harmful, the committee claims, public policies should take into account its influence.

As you read, consider the following questions:
1. According to the authors, why is focusing solely on limiting access to firearms a mistaken solution to violent juvenile crime?
2. In what way can television violence harm even young children, as stated by the authors?
3. In the author's opinion, in what ways are the effects of violent video games similar to those of violent television and film?

Senate Committee on the Judiciary, *Children, Violence, and the Media: A Report for Parents and Policy Makers*, September 14, 1999.

Americans have felt a growing and nagging uneasiness. . . . Yes, we have come to enjoy unparalleled material prosperity, personal freedom, and opportunity. And, yes, we live longer, healthier lives. Yet, for all these achievements, we also sense that our nation suffers from an insidious decay. Americans would hardly be surprised to learn that we lead the industrialized world in rates of murder, violent crime, juvenile crime, imprisonment, divorce, single-parent households, numbers of teen suicide, cocaine consumption, per capita consumption of all drugs, and pornography production.

The horrifying spate of school shootings between 1997 and 1999 has transformed that uneasiness into an almost desperate alarm. Behind the facade of our material comfort, we find a national tragedy: America's children are killing and harming each other. As Colorado Governor Bill Owens lamented in the wake of the Columbine High School massacre, on April 20, 1999, in Littleton, Colorado, a "virus" is loose within our culture, and that virus is attacking America's youth, our nation's most vulnerable and precious treasure.

Looking at the Statistics

The statistics are chilling. In 1997, law enforcement agencies in the United States arrested an estimated 2.8 million persons under age 18. Of that number, an estimated 2,500 juveniles were arrested for murder and 121,000 for other violent crimes. According to the FBI, juveniles accounted for 19% of all arrests, 14% of all murder arrests, and 17% of all violent crime arrests in 1997.

While the number of arrests of juveniles for violent crimes declined slightly from 1996 to 1997, the number of juvenile violent crime arrests in 1997 was still 49% above the 1988 level.

James Q. Wilson, one of our foremost experts on crime, has observed, "Youngsters are shooting at people at a far higher rate than at any time in recent history." The Centers for Disease Control and Prevention ("CDC") reports that a survey showed that some 5.9% of the American high school students surveyed said that they had carried a gun in the 30 days prior to the survey. Equally troubling, that survey also shows that 18% of high school students carry a knife, razor, firearm, or other weapon on a regular basis, and 9% of them take a weapon to school. While studies show that the amount of youth violence has started to decline, the CDC warns that "the prevalence of youth violence and school violence is still unacceptably high."

As a result of demographic trends, the problem of juvenile violence could dramatically worsen as the number of American teenagers will increase significantly over the next decade. According to Department of Justice estimates, the number of juveniles who will be arrested for violent crimes will double by the year 2010.

Finding a Solution

Fortunately, our nation's growing alarm carries with it a collective will for finding a solution. Americans know that something is wrong, and they are united in their desire to address the problem of youth violence. Americans also realize that a variety of factors underlie this national tragedy, including disintegrating nuclear families, child abuse and neglect, drug and alcohol abuse, a lack of constructive values, a revolving-door juvenile justice system, and pervasive media violence. Only a comprehensive approach that targets all of these factors has any hope of success, and Americans look to their elected leaders not for demagoguery or partisanship, but for effective legislation and empowering public policies.

Those who would focus solely on the instrumentalities children use to cause harm surely are mistaken. After all, there are unlimited ways that a child bent on violence can harm another person. Thus, limiting the access of troubled children to firearms and other weapons is but one aspect of a comprehensive approach. The remainder of that approach must address this question: Why does a child turn to violence?

A growing body of research concludes that media violence constitutes one significant part of the answer. With respect to television violence alone, a 1993 report by University of Washington epidemiologist Brandon S. Centerwall expresses a startling finding: "[If], hypothetically, television technology had never been developed, there would be 10,000 fewer homicides each year in the United States, 70,000 fewer rapes, and 700,000 fewer injurious assaults. Violent crime would be half what it is." Plainly, any solution to the juvenile violence problem that fails to address media violence is doomed to failure.

The Media Are Violent

American media are exceedingly violent. With television, analysis of programming for 20 years (1973 to 1993) found that over the years, the level of violence in prime-time programming remained at about 5 violent acts per hour. An August 1994 report by the Center for Media and Public Affairs reported that in one 18-hour day in 1992, observing 10 channels of all major kinds of programs, 1,846 different scenes of violence were noted, which translated to more than 10 violent scenes per hour, per channel, all day. A follow-up study conducted in 1994, found a 41% increase in violent scenes to 2,605, which translated to almost 15 scenes of violence per hour. Like television, our cinemas are full of movies that glamorize bloodshed and violence, and one need only listen to popular music radio and stroll down the aisle of almost any computer store to see that our music and video games are similarly afflicted.

Not only are our media exceedingly violent; they are also ubiquitous. The percentage of households with more than one television set has reached an all-time high of 87%, and roughly ½ of American children have a television set in their room. Forty-six percent of all homes with children have access to at least one television set, a VCR, home video game equipment and a personal computer, and 88.7% of such homes have either home video game equipment, a personal computer, or both.

What does that mean for our children? Most children now have unprecedented technological avenues for accessing the "entertainment" our media industries provide. The average 7th grader watches about 4 hours of television per day, and 60% of those shows contain some violence. The average 7th grader plays electronic games at least 4 hours per week, and 50% of those games are violent. According to the American Psychiatric Association, by age 18 an American child will have seen 16,000 simulated murders and 200,000 acts of violence.

The Littleton, Colorado, school massacre has spawned a national debate over how to respond to this culture of media violence. In May 1999, a *USA Today*/CNN/Gallup poll found that 73% of Americans believe that TV and movies are partly to blame for juvenile crime. A *Time*/CNN poll found that 75% of teens 13 to 17 years of age believe the Internet is partly responsible for crimes like the Littleton shootings, 66% blame violence in movies, television, and music, and 56% blame video game violence.

Horsey. © 1999 by *Seattle Post-Intelligencer*. Reprinted by special permission of King Features Syndicate.

In response, many, including the President, have called for studies to determine what effect that culture has on our children. Yet, we should not use such studies to dodge our responsibility to the American people. At least with respect to television and movies, existing research already demonstrates a solid link between media violence and the violent actions of our youth. Dr. Leonard D. Eron, a senior research scientist and professor of psychology at the University of Michigan, has estimated that television alone is responsible for 10% of youth violence. "The debate is over," begins a position paper on media violence by the American Psychiatric Association, "[f]or the last three decades, the one predominant finding in research on the mass media is that exposure to media portrayals of violence increases aggressive behavior in children." In the words of Jeffrey McIntyre, legislative and federal affairs officer for the American Psychological Association, "To argue against it is like arguing against gravity."

Television and Film Violence

It has been estimated that more than 1,000 studies on the effects of television and film violence have been done during the past 40 years. In the last decade the American Medical Association, the American Academy of Pediatrics, the American Academy of Child and Adolescent Psychiatry, and the National Institute of Mental Health have separately reviewed many of these studies. Each of these reviews has reached the same conclusion: television violence leads to real-world violence. The National Institute of Mental Health reported that "television violence is as strongly correlated with aggressive behavior as any variable that has been measured." A comprehensive study conducted by the Surgeon General's Office in 1972, and updated in 1982, found television violence a contributing factor to increases in violent crime and antisocial behavior; a 1984 United States Attorney General's Task Force study on family violence revealed that viewing television violence contributed to acting-out violence in the home; and recently, the National Television Violence Study, a 3-year project that examined the depiction of violent behavior across more than 8,200 programs, concluded that televised violence teaches aggressive attitudes and behaviors, desensitization to violence, and increased fear of becoming victimized by violence. The majority of the existing social and behavioral science studies, taken together, agree on the following basic points: (1) constant viewing of televised violence has negative effects on human character and attitudes; (2) television violence encourages violent forms of behavior and influences moral and social values about violence in daily life; (3) children who watch significant amounts of television violence have a greater likelihood of exhibiting later aggressive behavior; (4) television violence affects viewers of all ages, intellect, socioeconomic levels, and both genders; and (5) viewers who watch significant amounts of television violence perceive a meaner world and overestimate the possibility of being a victim of violence.

Drawing Conclusions

The research has also shown that television violence can harm even young children. Researchers have performed longitudinal studies of the impact of television violence on young children as they mature into adults. One such study, begun in 1960, examined 600 people at age 8, age 18, and age 30. The researchers concluded that boys at age 8 who had been watching more television violence than other boys grew up to be more aggressive than other boys, and they also grew up to be more aggressive and violent than one would have expected them to be on the basis of how aggressive they were as 8-year-olds. A second similar study, which included girls, arrived at a similar conclusion: children who watched more violence behaved more aggressively the next year than those who watched less violence on television, and more aggressively than anticipated based on their behavior the previous year. Professor L. Rowell Huesmann, one of the researchers behind these studies, summarized his findings before a Senate committee earlier this year:

> Not every child who watches a lot of violence or plays a lot of violent games will grow up to be violent. Other forces must converge, as they did recently in Colorado. But just as every cigarette increases the chance that someday you will get lung cancer, every exposure to violence increases the chances that some day a child will behave more violently than they otherwise would.

Some experts also believe that children can become addicted to violence. "Violence is like the nicotine in cigarettes," states Lieutenant Colonel Dave Grossman, a former Green Beret and West Point psychology professor who now heads the Killology Research Group. "The reason why the media has to pump ever more violence into us is because we've built up a tolerance. In order to get the same high, we need ever-higher levels. . . . The television industry has gained its market share through an addictive and toxic ingredient."

Not surprisingly, many have come to view television and

film violence as a national public health problem. The American Academy of Pediatrics, for instance, recently published a report advocating a national media education program to mitigate the negative impact of the harmful media messages seen and heard by children and adolescents. Robert Lichter, president of the Center for Media and Public Affairs, a nonprofit research group in Washington, D.C., has framed the issue in language we can all understand: "If you're worried about what your kid eats, you should worry about what your kid's watching."

Less research has been done on the effect of music, video games, and the Internet on children. Nonetheless, on the basis of both that research and the research findings concerning television and film, experts confidently predict that violent music, video games, and Internet material also will be found to have harmful effects on children.

The Influence of Violent Music

Few would doubt the overall effect music has on people. In Plato's *Republic*, Socrates said that "musical training is a more potent instrument than any other, because rhythm and harmony find their way into the inward places of the soul, on which they mightily fasten." Music affects our moods, our attitudes, our emotions, and our behavior; we wake to it, dance to it, and sometimes cry to it. From infancy it is an integral part of our lives.

As virtually any parent with a teenager can attest, music holds an even more special place in the hearts and minds of our young people. Academic studies confirm this wisdom. One survey of 2,760 14-to-16-year-olds in 10 different cities found that they listened to music an average of 40 hours per week. Research has also shown that the average teenager listens to 10,500 hours of rock music during the years between the 7th and 12th grades.

Inadequate attention has been paid to the effect on children of violent music lyrics. Although no studies have documented a cause-and-effect relationship between violent lyrics and aggressive behavior, studies do indicate that a preference for heavy metal music may be a significant marker for alienation, substance abuse, psychiatric disorders, suicide risk, sex-role stereotyping, or risk-taking behaviors during adolescence. In addition, a Swedish study has found that adolescents who developed an early interest in rock music were more likely to be influenced by their peers and less influenced by their parents than older adolescents.

With good reason, then, parents are concerned about the music lyrics their children hear. And parents should be concerned. Despite historic, bipartisan remedial legislation by the state and federal governments, it is stunning even to the casual listener how much modern music glorifies acts of violence. Studies show that modern music lyrics have become increasingly explicit, particularly concerning sex, drugs, and, most troubling, violence against women. For example, the rock band Nine Inch Nails released a song titled "Big Man with a Gun," which triumphantly describes a sexual assault at gun point. Such hatred and violence against women are widespread and unmistakable in mainstream hip-hop and alternative music. Consider the singer "Marilyn Manson," whose less vulgar lyrics include: "Who says date rape isn't kind?"; "Let's just kill everyone and let your god sort them out"; and "The housewife I will beat, the pro-life I will kill." Other Manson lyrics cannot be repeated here. Or consider Eminem, the hip-hop artist featured frequently on MTV, who recently wrote "Bonnie and Clyde," a song in which he described killing his child's mother and dumping her body in the ocean. . . .

We must not ignore the fact that these violent, misogynist images may ultimately affect the behavior and attitudes of many young men toward women. Writing about such lyrics in 1996, William J. Bennett, Senator Joseph Lieberman, and C. DeLores Tucker posed the following question: "What would you do if you discovered that someone was encouraging your sons to kill people indiscriminately, to find fun in beating and raping girls, and to use the word 'motherf—er' at least once in every sentence?" While the authors directed that question specifically to parents, it is best addressed to all Americans.

Examining Video Games and the Internet

Interactive video games and the Internet have become the entertainment of choice for America's adolescents. Nearly seven in ten homes with children now have a personal computer (68.2%), and 41% of homes with children have access to the Internet. Annual video game revenues in the United States exceed $10 billion, nearly double the amount of money Americans spend going to the movies. On average, American children who have home video game machines play with them about 90 minutes a day.

The video games of choice for our youth are those that contain depictions of violence. A 1993 study, for instance, asked 357 seventh- and eighth-graders to select their preferences among five categories of video games. Thirty-two percent of the children selected the category "fantasy violence," and 17% selected "human violence." Only 2% of the children chose "educational games."

Parents are concerned that the fantasy violence in video games could lead their children to real-world violence. That concern intensified when Americans learned that the two juveniles responsible for the Littleton massacre had obsessively played the ultra-violent video game "Doom." Americans also recalled that the 14-year-old boy who shot eight classmates in Paducah, Kentucky, in 1997, had been an avid player of video games. As the *New York Times* observed, "the search for the cause in the Littleton shootings continues, and much of it has come to focus on violent video games."

The Troubling Effects of Video Games

Here, too, the concern of parents is justified. Studies indicate that violent video games have an effect on children similar to that of violent television and film. That is, prolonged exposure of children to violent video games increases the likelihood of aggression. Some authorities go even further, concluding that the violent actions performed in playing video games are even more conducive to aggressive behavior. According to this view, the more often children practice fantasy acts of violence, the more likely they are to carry out real-world violent acts. As Professor Brian Stonehill, creator of the media studies program at Pomona College in Claremont, California, states: "The technology is going from passive to active. The violence is no longer vicarious with interactive media. It's much more pernicious and worrisome."

Another researcher characterizes such games as sophisti-cated simulators, similar to those used in military training.

Equally troubling, video games often present violence in a glamorized light. Typical games cast players in the role of a shooter, with points scored for each "kill." Furthermore, advertising for such games often touts the violent conduct as a selling point—the more graphic and extreme, the better. For example, the advertisement for the game "Destrega" reads: "Let the slaughter begin"; and for the game "Sub-space," "Meet people from all over the world, then kill them." As the popularity and graphic nature of such games increase, so does the harm to our youth. As Lt. Col. Dave Grossman bluntly warns, "We're not just teaching kids to kill. We're teaching them to like it.". . .

The effect of media violence on our children is no longer open to debate. Countless studies have shown that a steady diet of television, movie, music, video game, and Internet vi-olence plays a significant role in the disheartening number of violent acts committed by America's youth. We must now devote ourselves to reducing the amount and degree of vio-lence in our media and to shielding our children from such harmful depictions.

"As for making the explicit connection between on-screen mayhem . . . and real-life singular, serial or mass murder, scientific psychology . . . has simply not delivered the goods."

No Link Between Media Violence and Youth Violence Has Been Established

Stuart Fischoff

In the following viewpoint, originally given as a speech at the 1999 Annual Convention of the American Psychological Association, Stuart Fischoff contends that studies purportedly establishing a causal link between media and real-world violence cannot predict actual behavior. Media-violence researchers can make educated guesses about human behavior outside the lab, but because it would be unethical to include real violence in research studies, the question of whether media violence causes real-world violence can never be known. Fischoff is a professor of psychology at California State University, Los Angeles.

As you read, consider the following questions:
1. In Fischoff's opinion, under what circumstances is it especially important that researchers make valid generalizations of their lab results to the real world?
2. According to Fischoff, what are some of the aggressive behaviors used as dependent variables in media-violence research?

Stuart Fischoff, "Psychology's Quixotic Quest for the Media-Violence Connection," *Journal of Media Psychology*, vol. 4, Fall 1999. Copyright © 1999 by *Journal of Media Psychology*. Reproduced by permission.

*T*he plethoric effluence of screen violence, murder and mayhem is an undisputed menace to society.

That's the message from such sources as President Bill Clinton, Congressman Henry Hyde, Senator Joseph Lieberman, both APAs [the American Psychological Association and the American Psychiatric Association], The American Academy of Pediatrics, Congressional committees and Surgeon General reports.

These denunciations are clear and, for most Americans and most psychologists, intuitively obvious and obviously true.

Yes, the snack counter availability of guns and the National Rifle Association (NRA) defenders of the right to market and bear these snacks are a problem.

Yes, poverty, teenage alienation, lack of parental involvement with transmitting proper social values and behaviors to their children is a problem.

Yes, a culture which is steeped in materialism and conspicuous consumption and which judges one's worth as a person by one's economic worth is a vexing issue.

And, yes, drug and gang-related crime is a problem.

Pointing the Finger

But, if the amount of devoted newshole space, the number of "scientific" studies done over 50 years, and the number of pronouncements, advisories, and appeals issued by professional and lay organizations is any indication, if we can just get a handle on violence in film and television, our "shining city on the Hill" [Washington, D.C.], would be launched on the road to salvation.

The trouble with all these political and scientifically based pronouncements, nostrums, and admonitions is that what is obvious is not always true and what is true is not always obvious.

For years, interminably and predictably, Hollywood vigorously denied or sidestepped the charge that the violence on movie and TV screens is a major cause of real-life violence. Hollywood questioned the research supporting the causal connection between media violence and real-life violence, and diverted attention from its hegemonic entertainment machine to drugs, single-parent families, absentee, negligent or materialistically obsessed parents, the NRA, or to other social institutions. When all else failed, Hollywood wrapped itself around the flag of First Amendment freedoms of the press and of speech and raised the clarion cry of creative freedom.

Of late, however, especially in the wake of the sense-defying massacre on April 20, 1999, at Columbine High School, in Littleton, Colorado, such verbal sleight of hand is falling on cynical ears. The drums along the Potomac are beating ever louder and Hollywood is running out of First Amendment whining turf and out of the compromise turf of the current film rating system. The film and TV folk in Hollywood are running for cover. Finger pointing . . . has already begun.

An Easy Target

There are, of course, many other factors that contribute to violence in general and Columbine violence in particular. But they embrace social forces, which are far more difficult to manage. These are socially and politically desperate, perilous and opportunistic times. Media-manufactured violence is an easier and, in truth, a slower moving target. And Congress is taking dead aim.

Because of our belief in the media-violence connection, we are primed to search for the usual suspects. What movies did the trigger men at Columbine High School, Eric Harris and Dylan Kleibold, see before they mounted their assault? What were their favorite TV shows and video games and music genres? They saw *The Matrix* or *Basketball Diaries*? They own Mortal Kombat? They listen to gangsta' rap. Bam! That's the answer. The media did it. The fact that they were neo-Nazis, had arrest records, were on prescriptive drugs, and were treated by counselors for their anger and aggressiveness somehow, for many, got lost in the shuffle of feet looking for easy answers—media answers.

Paradoxically, though, Hollywood's defense of itself by questioning the research behind the charges that it inspires such violent acts as Columbine may, in fact, be quite on the money, although probably asserted for dubious and self-serving reasons. Even if Hollywood was not the slow moving target that it is, does the scientific literature actually support the connection between violence portrayed in the entertainment media and violence enacted in real life? More pointedly, does extant scientific research in this area help us, in any way whatsoever, to predict or prevent events like the Columbine?

Let us call this alleged link between media portrayals of violence and real-world viewer violence the "media-violence connection." What does the research literature actually say about this connection?

Failing to Connect Media and Real-Life Violence

After 50 years and over 1,000 studies (a conservative estimate), there is, I submit, not a single research study which is even remotely predictive of the Columbine massacre or similar high school shootings. Yes, there may be research which may predict fights on school yard grounds and may account for teenage aggression in the streets and spousal abuse after televised prize fights (and much research which argues the other way; research which you rarely hear about). But as for making the explicit connection between on-screen mayhem by the bodies of Sylvester Stallone and Arnold Schwarzenegger, the minds of Oliver Stone and Wes Craven, and real-life singular, serial or mass murder, scientific psychology, albeit noble and earnest in its tireless efforts, has simply not delivered the goods. It asserts the causal nexus but doesn't actually demonstrate it.

The paucity of research evidence doesn't stop with connecting media violence to murderous rampages. There are dozens of studies, which suggest that watching sexually violent movies desensitize males to the plight of rape victims. These studies further allege that, as a consequence of viewing sexually violent material, males are more likely to acquit a rapist or assign more blame to a rape victim (or even be more likely to commit rape themselves).

Abhorrent as what I have to say may be, however, I believe that there is not a single study that is externally valid because there is not a single study that has explored such supposed post-exposure rape attitudes in an even quasi-decent jury simulation setting or gained the cooperation of the courts to

31

test the desensitization hypothesis in a real juridical setting. All the arguments about desensitization have come from lab situations with subjects reading transcripts or watching videotapes of real or simulated testimony.

To argue that because subjects in a lab situation displayed desensitization to violence we can safely predict that non-quiche-eating real men, watching sexually violent films in real theaters or in real homes are more likely to acquit a real-life rapist in a real jury setting is a psychologically huge and untested leap of faith. The leap suggesting that such men will be more likely to rape someone is even more chasmic and, I think, professionally irresponsible. And the leap from so-called aggressive behavior in a lab setting to murder in real life is just as, how shall I say it? Loony.

The importance of the question of external validity, i.e., valid generalizations to the real world, is monumental when it comes to taking lab results about acquisition of violent attitudes, values or behaviors or about desensitization to sexually violent behavior and predicting real world behavior. It is especially important when the results of such research are used as the basis for advocating or passing socially restrictive government legislation. . . .

A Tendency to Overgeneralize

The sad truth is that psychologists are on a perpetual and reckless tear when it comes to predicting social disease dynamics based on laboratory-observed symptoms. But this is nothing new.

Gordon Allport in his APA presidential address foreshadowed a deep concern for psychologists' tendency to overgeneralize their laboratory and field research over 50 years ago. Former APA president Ronald Fox paraphrased Allport in a 1996 *American Psychologist* article:

"Allport believed that psychology did not have the proper frame of reference to be able to predict, understand, and control human behavior. Our inability to make meaningful predictions about individual behavior, Allport believed, stems from an overreliance on methodologies that neither take direct experience as a model for its constructs nor return to that experience for validation of its results. In order to predict critical behaviors, one must actually deal with those behaviors, not with analogues or overly simplified imitations that bear little resemblance to the real thing. Allport urged the study of the actual behaviors that are of pressing social significance, at a suitable level of complexity, and then the verification of predictions by the actual lives men lead."

Why, like the ghost of Hamlet's father, are Allport's concerns 50 years ago still haunting the ivory castles of academia today? Because legitimate caution about problems of external validity in media-violence research has been buried under an avalanche of crisis-driven, politically correct and philosophically driven research and research funding that speaks the speech that people and politicians want to hear—violent media causes violent behavior. . . .

An Absurd Conclusion

The drumbeat of political correctness on this issue is professionally exasperating. On a regular basis tawdry whores of designs and conclusions pass for elegant ladies of scientific respectability. Let me provide an example. I recently agreed to do a review and analysis of a highly touted research article (the media was all over it), about media and violence. The request came from *The Forensic Echo*, a newsmagazine of psychiatry, law and public policy.

I won't burden you with the morass of conceptual and methodological outrages perpetrated by the research design which totally undercut the validity of its conclusion which, not surprisingly, affirmed the media-violence connection. I would just point out that the operationally defined measure of aggression in the study was the willingness of the college student subjects to recommend against renewal of the research grant of a research Director and her assistant. This display of so-called aggression occurred after the experimental procedure had openly deceived the subjects and held them hostage to their promised reward by cutting short the experiment they had signed on for, and demanding they participate in another experiment. After this forced experimental march, the Director had roundly insulted their performance and abused their intelligence.

At various places in the discussion and conclusions of the

article, the terms violence, aggression and hostility were used interchangeably. Finally, the authors concluded that the study had demonstrated the long-term effects (viewing four violent movies in four days) of media violence exposure on aggressive behavior. What!!!

Where Children Really Learn Violence

Despite the lack of evidence, politicians can't resist blaming the media for violence. They can stake out the moral high ground confident that the First Amendment will protect them from having to actually write legislation that would be likely to alienate the entertainment industry. Some use the issue as a smokescreen to avoid having to confront gun control.

But violence isn't learned from mock violence. There is good evidence—causal evidence, not correlational—that it's learned in personal violent encounters, beginning with the brutalization of children by their parents or their peers.

Richard Rhodes, *New York Times*, September 17, 2000.

What can we say about such academic absurdity and scientific word salad? Are aggression, violence and hostility synonyms? If so, we have too much redundancy in our language. Is recommending non-renewal of a grant the kind of hostility we're concerned about in America today? Are four violent movies in four days really "long term effects of violence exposure?" I don't think so. What can we say about the reviewers of the article? What can we say about the journal, which published the article? The same journal, incidentally, which only recently published my own article.

What the Research Does Show

I should point out here that it is not that I believe that media violence DOESN'T produce violent behavior in viewers, or in some viewers or in 5–10% of viewers as Leonard Eron, Nancy Signorelli and others have recently come to believe after decades of asserting before Congress or in other venues, that media violence is a principal cause of real-world violence. I am merely asserting that the connection between the two has not been empirically established.

Psychologist Rowell Huesmann has said not that media

violence produces violent behavior in 5–10% of the viewers, but that it accounts for 5–10% of the variance in viewer violence. Now, is that 5–10% of violence the violence we see in schoolyards, between sibs, in drive-by shootings or in the slaughter at Columbine? And how on earth does anyone really know that media violence accounts for 5–10% of real-world violence? Based on the square of .30 correlations in field or lab studies? And what sort of aggressive behavior is that which we are dealing with in lab studies? Specifically, what are the critical dependent variables?

A look at the hundreds if not thousands of published and unpublished lab and field studies suggests several classes of aggressive behavior are the usual dependent variable suspects:

1. Assaulting dolls
2. Administering shock
3. School yard fighting
4. Aggressive thoughts
5. Recommending grant terminations

The only study of which I'm aware which purportedly dealt with real violent crime was the Huesmann and Eron study on cumulative effects of TV watching and real-world criminality. In their study, however, watching violent TV did not correlate with real-world violence or criminality when measured concurrently at ages 8 and 30. No, it correlated with violence watching at eight and criminal behavior at 30. In effect, media exposure created scripts not impulses. Thus, there were no short-term, only long-term correlates of media violence watching and anti-social behavior? Yet, if we consider the arguments cited in the popular press and in many text books, the violent behavior in response to viewing violent TV or film fare is short-fused. Thus, the conclusions of the only long-duration, naturalistic study of media and violence flies in the face of the wisdom dispensed in many psychology text books and lay advocates of legislatively mandated or voluntary media control.

A Need for Answers

As a profession, do we dare recommend legislation designed to control school massacres when our dependent variables in research are generally so benign, so lacking in external validity for the target behaviors that so concern us? Are we really possessed of such professional hubris that we advocate such restraints on civil liberties when our scientific database is so dubious? Obviously we do and we are. . . .

The current violence in society is disturbing to all of us. The current excessive, gratuitous violence in film, in video games, in music lyrics is disturbing to all of us. But because two phenomena are both disturbing and coincident in time does not make them causally connected, any more than the correlation between ice cream consumption and drowning can be understood as yielding a causal nexus. So, let us all beware.

Yet, we are intent on making this media-violence connection, this "fundamedia attribution error." Politicians and psychologists cite thousands of studies that have, to use Rowell Huesmann's words, "provided incontrovertible evidence of the strong media-violence connection."

Well, let me suggest again that the evidence for this vaunted connection is very controvertible. Whether we cite 100, 1,000, or 10,000 research studies which conclude that exposure to violent media produces violent behavior, 10,000 is no more persuasive or credible than 100, if the designs of the research are flawed and/or the generalizations to an external population of behaviors are patently unjustified.

The Ethics of Experimentation

So, you ask, why not just do the necessary research in controlled settings and see if exposure to violent movies produces real-world type violence, not just benign, ersatz violent behaviors like those listed above? The simple answer is, we can't. We can't and we don't because ethical guidelines at all American universities explicitly prohibit the conduct of real violence in experimental settings or, by deception, getting human subjects to do things about which they might later feel intense guilt.

There are, of course, certain things you can ethically do in an experiment. You can show a subject filmed violence and ask him if he would be more likely to commit similar aggression if someone insulted him. You can even give him the opportunity, after watching some violent footage, to administer (supposed) shock to an opponent in some competitive contest after the opponent angered him. You can even get him or her to pummel a Bobo doll.

But what researchers cannot do is show a subject ten violent movies and see if he will pick up a gun and shoot another subject who has insulted him or "dissed" his saintly mother (even if, in reality, there are only blanks in the gun). Consequently, laboratory expressions of violence lack external validity, i.e., they simply do not generalize to or predict events like Columbine.

There's the rub: Our vaunted scientific research machine is stymied when it comes to investigating the sorts of aggressive behaviors that we, as a culture, are most concerned about. To suggest we have accomplished this task based on the dependent variables we have used in previous studies is the moral and logical equivalent of marketing a drug for cancer which research has shown cures acne. . . .

In effect, it is time to stop offering explanations for social behavior that our research designs are actually unable to investigate and therefore are unable to address. We can offer educated opinions but we can't offer anything even approaching incontrovertible proof of these opinions. Can you imagine doing medical research on drugs or other treatments for life-threatening illnesses without doing long-term clinical trials?

If we want to control our popular culture and our crime, we had better do the right studies with the right populations, in the right conditions, over the right period of time before we hand out cultural prescriptions and proscriptions at congressional hearings and in our classrooms. I abhor the gratuitous media violence in film, in video games, on TV as much as you do. I think it produces an ugly cultural landscape, a landscape littered with the trash and the psychological graffiti of egocentric or puerile minds, minds that put the value of money and convenience above the value of a livable, sustainable physical and social environment.

I believe the roots of social violence lie in our social values about what's important in life, what sustains us as a culture, not what drives us as an economy. I believe we need to pay more than lip service when we say our children are our future and then buy their quiet and quiet their demands for parenting with credit cards, cell phones or electronic baby or child sitters like televisions, computers and internet access. Conceiving children can be a mindless, biological act; parenting is always a mindful, psychological commitment. Too often we see people embrace the first and abandon the second. When that happens, the specter of the "tyranny of the peer group" raises its perilous head. And if we wonder what that will yield, the Trench Coat Mafia and the Lords of Chaos* offer a vivid reminder.

*The Trench Coat Mafia is the name applied to a group of "outcasts" at Columbine High School. Some of the early members wore black trench coats. Eric Harris and Dylan Klebold were identified as members of the organization, which had no formal structure. The Lords of Chaos consisted of a group of teenaged friends whose goal was to "cause chaos and destruction." They began their crime spree with acts of vandalism and arson and, in April 1996, murdered a high school band director.

> "The [National Institute of Mental Health]
> report concluded that exposure to television
> violence contributes to aggressive behavior
> in children."

Exposure to Television Violence Is Harmful

Stacy L. Smith and Edward Donnerstein

According to Stacy L. Smith and Edward Donnerstein in the following viewpoint, a significant amount of television programming is violent. Unfortunately, research reveals that exposure to violent television content is harmful, the authors contend. For example, some of those exposed to television violence learn aggressive behavior, others become desensitized to violence, and still others have exaggerated fears of becoming a victim of violence, according to the authors. Smith is a professor at Michigan State University. Donnerstein directs the Center for Communication and Social Policy at the University of California, Santa Barbara, and is coeditor of *Human Aggression: Theories, Research, and Implications for Social Policy*, from which the following viewpoint is taken.

As you read, consider the following questions:

1. According to Smith and Donnerstein, what three trends in American television viewing habits were revealed by research on television exposure?
2. What differences emerged when the authors examined the prevalence of violence across different channels and genre types?

Stacy L. Smith and Edward Donnerstein, "Harmful Effects of Exposure to Media Violence: Learning of Aggression, Emotional Desensitization, and Fear," *Human Aggression: Theories, Research, and Implications for Social Policy*, edited by Russell G. Geen and Edward Donnerstein. New York: Academic Press, 1998. Copyright © 1998 by Academic Press. Reproduced by permission of Harcourt.

A merica is a violent country. The statistics on crime and violence in the United States are staggering, particularly regarding children and adolescents. For example, consider the following figures cited by the American Psychological Association (1993) and U.S. Department of Justice (1997):

- Every 5 min a child is arrested for a violent crime.
- Adolescents account for 24% of all violent crimes leading to arrest. This rate has increased over time for 12 to 19 year olds and is down for individuals 35 and older.
- Every day over 100,000 children carry guns to school.
- Nearly 9 million 12 to 17 year olds have seen someone being shot with a gun, knifed, sexually assaulted, mugged, robbed, or threatened with a weapon during their lifetime.
- Gun-related violence takes the life of an American child every 3 hr.
- Among individuals 15 to 24 years old, homicide is the second leading cause of death. For African-Americans in this age bracket, however, it is number one.
- A child growing up in Chicago is 15 times more likely to be murdered than a child growing up in Northern Ireland.

Explaining Trends in Violence

What accounts for these alarming trends? Violent and criminal behavior is the result of a multiplicity of factors such as gang membership, drug and alcohol use, gun availability, poverty, brain damage, impulsivity, and racism, among many others. Many of these variables may independently or interactively affect antisocial responding. Due to the complexity of these and many other contributory factors, groups such as the American Psychological Association (APA), American Medical Association (AMA), National Academy of Science (NAS), and Centers for Disease Control (CDCP), have all examined extensively the multiple causes of aggression in society. Cutting across all these investigations was a profound realization that the mass media, particularly television and film violence, also contributes to antisocial behavior in our country.

We realize that media violence is not the sole cause of aggressive behavior. We also recognize that media violence is not the only or even the most important cause of antisocial actions. Furthermore, it is not every violent act on television or film that is of concern. Nor will every child or adult act aggressively after watching a violent media portrayal. However, there is clear evidence that exposure to media violence contributes in significant ways to violence in our society. . . .

Exposure to Television

Americans are fascinated with television. Indeed, a full 98% of the homes in this country have one television set and nearly 66% have two or more. Of those homes that own at least one television, over 65% subscribe to cable programming and approximately two thirds own a VCR. In most U.S. households, the television set is "on" an average of 7 hr per day and over 8 hr per day for those households that subscribe to cable. These figures reveal that the television set in the "average" American home is "on" approximately 50–64 hr per week!

Given these statistics, how much time do individuals actually spend watching television? Nielsen ratings for the first quarter of the 1996 season revealed that individuals 18 and over are watching an average of 32 hr of television a week with women (34 hr a week) viewing slightly more than men (30 hr a week). Thus, the average adult spends over 4 hr per day watching TV, which is more time spent on any one activity outside of working or sleeping.

Viewing Habits

Surprisingly, children spend slightly less time viewing television than do adults. Nielsen ratings for the first quarter of the 1996 viewing season revealed that 2 to 11 year olds spend an average of 22 hr per week watching television whereas 12 to 17 year olds spend an average of 20 hr per week viewing television. Even more conservative estimates suggest that children spend 2–3 hr viewing television per day. Similar to adults, these statistics indicate that America's youth also spend a great deal of their leisure time in front of the TV. Indeed, a national survey of 1228 parents and their children reveals that after sleeping, 2 to 17 year olds spend more time watching television than doing homework, reading books, using a computer, playing video games, or reading magazines or newspapers.

Viewing estimates for children from specific subgroups of the population are even higher. For instance, J.P. Tangey and S. Feshbach (1988) assessed the impact of several demographic variables on television viewing across three different samples of older elementary school-aged children. Across all three groups, results revealed that African-American children watch nearly twice as much television per week as Caucasian children, independent of parents' level of education. Other studies have revealed that children from low-income families watch substantially more television than do children from mid- to high-income families. Clearly, children who come from some of the most vulnerable subgroups of the population are the heaviest viewers of television, presumably due to their lack of alternative activities.

In total, the research reviewed reveals three major trends in Americans' television viewing habits. First, individuals in this country are heavy consumers of television programming. Second, adults spend a great deal of time watching television in general and they seem to be "modeling" their viewing habits to the children of this country. Third, children are also heavy viewers of television, particularly if they come from African-American or poor families.

Studying Violence on American Television

With a steady viewing diet of 2–3 hr of television per day, how much violence are children being exposed to? Researchers have estimated that by the time a child finishes elementary school, he/she will have seen approximately 8000 murders and over 100,000 other acts of violence on TV. These figures are significantly higher for youngsters who are heavy viewers of television or who have access to premium cable programming or violent films they can rent or buy and watch on a VCR.

Several content analyses over the last three decades have been conducted to systematically assess the prevalence of violence on television. The largest and most rigorous of these was undertaken by 10 researchers (i.e., Barbara Wilson, Dale Kunkel, Daniel Linz, Edward Donnerstein, James Potter, Stacy Smith, Eva Blumenthal, Tim Gray, Michael Berry, and Carolyn Colvin) at the University of California, Santa Barbara. Working under the auspices of the National Television Violence Study (NTVS), these scholars were funded by the National Cable Television Association to examine longitudinally the amount and context of violence on American television for 3 consecutive years. . . .

What is the prevalence of violence on American television? Results from the first-year NTVS report reveal that a full 57% of programs on television contain some violence. Over 8000 violent scenes and 18,000 violent interactions spanned the entire sample, with 66% of those interactions including behavioral acts of violence, 29% involving credible threats of violence, and 3% involving harmful consequences of unseen violence. Only 4% of all violent programs on television feature an "antiviolence" theme. Put in another way, 96% of all violent television programs use aggression as a narrative, cinematic device for simply entertaining the audience. These prevalence findings are incredibly consistent across two randomly sampled composite weeks of television from 2 different years.

When we take a look at the prevalence of violence across different channels and genre types, some significant differences emerge. Comparing channel types to the industry average (57%), premium cable (85%) features substantially more programs with violence than broadcast networks (44%) and PBS (18%). In terms of genre types, movies (90%) and drama series (72%) contain significantly more violence than reality-based shows (30%) and comedies (27%).

The Way Violence Is Portrayed

Although the aforementioned results are interesting, they only inform us about the prevalence of violence on television. What should be of greater concern is the context or way in which violence is portrayed on TV. When we look more closely at the context of violence, the results reveal that most aggression on television is glamorized. Nearly one-half (44%) of the violent interactions on television involve perpetrators who have some attractive qualities worthy of emulation. Nearly 40% of the scenes involve humor either directed at the violence or used by characters involved with violence. Furthermore, a full 74% of all violent scenes on television feature no immediate punishment or condemnation for violence. Almost 40% of the programs feature "bad" characters who are never or rarely punished for their aggressive actions. These findings are also incredibly consistent across two composite weeks of television sampled over a 2-year period.

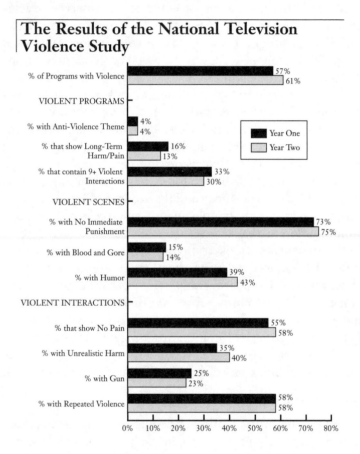

The Results of the National Television Violence Study

National Television Violence Study findings for the 1994–1995 and 1995–1996 television viewing seasons. From the Center for Communication and Social Policy, 1997, with permission.

Much of the violence on television is also sanitized. For example, over half of the violent behavioral interactions on television feature no pain (55%) and 47% feature no harm. A full 40% of the violent behavioral interactions depict harm in an unrealistic fashion with the greatest prevalence of unrealistic harm appearing in children's programming, presumably due to cartoons. Of all violent scenes on television, 86% feature *no* blood or gore. This is surprising given that nearly 40% of all interactions involved conventional weapons such as guns, knives, bombs, or other heavy weaponry! Finally, only 16% of violent programs featured the long-term, realistic consequences of violence. These findings are remarkably stable across a composite week of television randomly sampled from the 1994–1995 and 1995–1996 viewing seasons.

The NTVS is not without limitations, however. Perhaps one of the major drawbacks of this study was the decision to sample but *not* assess violence in news programs. Empirical research indicates that much of news programming is filled with stories about crime and violence. Approximately 15% of the programs on the broadcast networks and 10% of the programs on the independent stations are news, not to mention the two CNN channels on basic cable. Given that news stories often feature violence or its harmful aftermath, the prevalence of violence on American television may be considerably higher than the NTVS findings reveal. . . .

The findings from this massive study suggest two major trends in television programming: (a) violence is pervasive on television and (b) much of violence is glamorized and sanitized.

The Harmful Effects of Media Violence

If individuals are exposed to television content that is filled with portrayals of violence, what effect is it having on children, adolescents, and adults? In a poll of 600 adults conducted by *Time* and CNN, many Americans believe that violence contributes to harmful effects on viewers. Three quarters of those surveyed said that violence in television, movies, and music videos inspires young people to act violently. Furthermore, a full 76% of those interviewed stated that it numbs individuals to violence so that they are insensitive or calloused to it. These figures suggest that many Americans believe that exposure to media violence contributes to a range of antisocial effects on viewers.

Over the years, several governmental and professional organizations have conducted exhaustive reviews of the scientific literature to ascertain the relationship between exposure to media violence and aggressive behavior. These investigations have documented consistently that exposure to media violence contributes to aggressive behaviors in viewers and may influence their perceptions and attitudes about violence in the real world.

The earliest of these investigations was conducted by the U.S. Surgeon General (1972). The Surgeon General funded several studies specifically designed to assess the impact of exposure to media violence on child and adolescent viewers. Research revealed that there was a significant correlation between viewing television violence and aggressive behavior. This finding emerged across several different measures of aggressive behavior (i.e., self-report, peer ratings) and across several different methodological approaches (i.e., correlational, cross-lagged longitudinal investigations) to studying the problem. Experimental evidence in the report also made it clear that there was a direct, causal link between exposure to television violence and subsequent aggressive behavior in child viewers.

Ten years later, the National Institute of Mental Health (1982) conducted a follow-up investigation to review and integrate research that had been undertaken since the Surgeon General's (1972) report. The NIMH (1982) report concluded that exposure to television violence contributes to aggressive behavior in children, completely supporting the conclusion reached in the Surgeon General's study. Only now, the relationship could be extended to also account for preschoolers and older adolescents, and was generalizable to both boys and girls. The NIMH report also revealed that there were other harmful effects associated with exposure to television violence. Studies had revealed that heavy exposure to television violence contributes to increased fear of becoming a victim of violence and exaggerated perceptions of how much aggression and criminal activity occur in the world.

Additional reports have lent further support to the mass media's harmful impact on the audience. For example, the CDCP (1991), the NAS (1993), the AMA (1996), and the

APA (1992) all examined the relationship between exposure to media violence and antisocial behavior. Of all these reports, the most comprehensive came from the APA in 1992. Establishing a commission on youth and violence, the APA committee reviewed five decades of scientific research on the causes and prevention of violence in society. Like previous investigations into violence, the role of the mass media was considered and the conclusions reached were strikingly similar to the NIMH and Surgeon General's report.

The Consequences of Exposure

After scouring hundreds of empirical studies, the commission arrived at several significant conclusions regarding the harmful effects of exposure to media violence. First, heavy viewing of media violence is correlated with aggressive behavior and increased aggressive attitudes. The correlation between viewing violence on television and exhibiting aggressive behavior is fairly stable over time, place, and demographics. Experimental and longitudinal studies also supported the position that viewing television violence is related causally to aggressive behavior. Even more important, naturalistic field studies and cross-national investigations reveal that viewing televised aggression leads to increases in subsequent aggression and that such behavior can become part of a lasting behavioral pattern.

The APA report stated that exposure to media violence at a young age can have lasting, long-life negative consequences. If aggressive habits are learned early in life, they may form the foundation for later antisocial behavior. For example, aggressive children who struggle academically and socially/interpersonally tend to watch more television. Viewing violence on television reinforces their aggressive tendencies, only increasing their social and academic failure. These effects may have both short- and long-term implications. Indeed, L.R. Huesmann and colleagues found a clear and significant relationship between early exposure to televised violence at age 8 and adult criminal behavior 22 years later.

The APA commission also concluded that exposure to television violence may alter individuals' attitudes and behaviors toward violence in two particular ways. First, prolonged viewing of media violence may emotionally desensitize viewers toward real world violence. As a result, individuals may develop calloused attitudes toward aggression directed at others and a decreased likelihood to take action on behalf of a victim when violence occurs.

Second, exposure to media violence can contribute to increased fear in viewers about becoming a victim of real world violence. As a result, individuals may become increasingly untrusting or suspicious of others and engage in a variety of self-protective behaviors. Research on the effects of cumulative exposure to television reveals that heavy viewers may develop attitudes and beliefs about the world that "match" or are very similar to the world presented on television. Because television is filled with stories about crime and violence, heavy viewing can contribute to developing exaggerated perceptions of how much violence occurs in this world or unrealistic fears and beliefs about becoming a victim of violence.

In total then, over four decades of social science research reveals that exposure to media violence contributes to many undesirable effects on the audience. Viewing television violence contributes to (a) learning aggressive thoughts, attitudes, and behaviors, (b) emotional desensitization to real world aggression and its victims, and (c) fear of becoming a victim of violence.

*"Television violence and real-world violence
. . . are not at all equivalent."*

The Dangers of Television Violence Are Exaggerated

Jib Fowles

According to Jib Fowles, a professor of communication at the University of Houston and author of *The Case for Television Violence*, from which the following viewpoint is taken, the dangers of television violence have been exaggerated. The practice of counting violent acts in television programming, he argues, says little about the relationship between television and real-world violence. Most people watch voluntarily, Fowles maintains, and can easily determine that television violence is not real. Although fears about television violence generate periods of public debate, people have historically enjoyed watching violent spectacles and many still do by watching violent television, he contends.

As you read, consider the following questions:
1. According to Fowles, what types of violent television programming do violence counters often ignore?
2. In what ways do television and real-world violence differ, in the author's opinion?
3. In Fowles's opinion, how do polarized terms for television, such as "vast wasteland" and the "boob tube," influence the media-violence debate?

B eavis and Butt-head, the flagrantly imbecilic cartooned teenagers who appeared daily on the youth-oriented MTV channel, managed to create a large dent in American culture between their debut in 1992 and their cancellation in 1997. They were hugely popular with youngsters, having twice the ratings of any other MTV offering. To the delight of child and adolescent viewers, the two characters flunked all their courses, started fires, picked their noses, denigrated reading, indulged in the few prerogatives of youthful lust, and so on, all the while cackling moronically. The same strident idiocy that made them so attractive to youngsters also necessarily repulsed their elders; of all television shows, this was the most frequently banned by parents.

Accusations Against Beavis and Butt-head

Perhaps pervasive adult revulsion was part of the reason that in October 1993 many people were quick to accept wire service accounts of a house fire and death supposedly prompted by Beavis and Butt-head's pyromania. After a 5-year-old Moraine, Ohio, boy set his family's mobile home ablaze, killing his 2-year-old sister in the process, their mother claimed he was imitating the cartoon pair. This matter did not end just with the news stories and the usually mild admonitions. The outcry that followed was so pronounced that MTV took action, ordering the show's creator, Mike Judge, to remove any allusions to matches and fires in upcoming episodes. Even this concession, however, did not quiet the adverse reaction, and a week later MTV announced it would eliminate the early evening broadcast of the show (while lengthening the 11:00 P.M. show). It seemed that the channel's executives had been quicker to censor the program than to alter its time slot; the first option had ethical but no financial consequences, whereas the second, resulting in smaller audience sizes, would certainly produce less advertising revenue. Mike Judge, dispirited by the turn of events, said wearily, "I've gotten so tired that I don't like fighting big battles."

The story of the Ohio fire appears to be a cautionary tale about the possible impact of televised misbehavior, a parable for the video age. A terrible tragedy had apparently resulted because a viewing child imitated a destructive act seen on the television screen. However, reporters' follow-up stories cast much doubt on the original version. The boy's family did not receive cable television and thus he could not have been a regular viewer of *Beavis and Butt-head*. He might have seen the program at nearby homes but for the fact that the entire trailer park was not wired for cable. According to neighbors, the little boy had been playing with matches for several years. The culpability of the fictional cretins dwindles to nought, however appealing it was in the search for scapegoats. . . .

Counting Violence

Television has had no shortage of assaultive characters such as Beavis and Butt-head. . . . Throughout the decades, various versions of Beavis and Butt-head's "frog baseball" (no description necessary) have popped up in the broadcast schedule, an expressive arena that has always resounded with thwacks, blasts, shots, pileups, punches, crunches, crashes, screams, and the occasional silent stabbing. Confronting this largess in what James Twitchell calls "concussive fictions," communication scientists early on began the apparently simple and straightforward task of tallying the number of violent acts on the medium. Continuities in violent content were to be met with continuities in research strategies.

At first, "violence counting" seemed to be an appropriate approach, one with dispassionate pretensions and the promise of robust findings. If done accurately—and in conception the research design did not seem intricate or formidable—such counts would have the ring of science to them and not be readily dismissible. It would only be later, on reflection, that violence counting became suspect. . . .

The long-standing practice of television violence counts documents what is obvious to all: The amount of violence on the screen has been and continues to be voluminous and intractable. Although the violence on highly visible networks' series is surely on the decline, the violence on the less scrutinized cable channels is surely on the rise. This shift in content parallels, and may be related to, the shift in respective audience sizes as the networks' share of the prime-time viewership decreases toward the 50% level (from more than 90% as recently as the 1970s) while the cable channels' portion rises. Overall, the total amount of fantasy violence delivered by the medium is at least steady and may well be climbing. According to one cross-cultural survey, it is more prevalent on American television than in representative Asian (Japan) and European (Spain) countries. Indisputably, scenes of violence predominate in the nation's favorite medium.

In addition to its repeated documentation of television's violence offerings, there are other continuities inherent in the violence count tradition—ones that are not so readily seen because they are subsurface and countervailing. From the 1950s to the present, this line of research, sturdy to all appearances, has been weakened by concealed defects serious enough for David Gauntlett (1995) to propose, "The view of many researchers that violence on television is something which can be simply counted up—an assumption shared by the popular press—has been of little help to the progress of meaningful research." There are four major flaws that obstruct "the progress of meaningful research."

The Flaws in Violence Counting

First, the very accuracy of the counts is suspect—not solely because of minor definitional quarrels but also for unexpected reasons, with unexpected consequences. Even taken on their own terms, the summations of hostile depictions on television undoubtedly represent undercounts of the actualities and not inflated figures. Violence counters typically do not view sports programming as pertinent, do not develop coding schemes for such content, and therefore ignore an extensive area of televised combat. Interpersonal contesting and aggression are the essence of sports and the attraction for each broadcast's tens of millions of viewers. It is clear that football, boxing, and wrestling are violent sports but so are basketball and baseball in more stylized forms. Even a game such as tennis, ostensibly genteel, is premised on interpersonal aggression—on its displacement to a ball smashed repeatedly with an implement; the grunts from the participants tell reflective spectators of the retaliatory exertion being expended. The vocabulary for televised athletic events, so common as to go unnoticed, is replete with assaultive expressions: hit, strike, attack, bat, tackle, clip, slam, shoot, drive, dominate.

Another order of televised entertainment is also drenched in aggression but . . . is almost never tallied. It is a particular cultural filter Americans possess that allows them not to perceive the hostility inherent in humor and in the highly developed television variety of it— the situation comedy. The most prevalent televised genre, with 46 of the 100 highest rated series of all time, situation comedies are everywhere construed as harmless and innocent, but on analysis they are revealed as thoroughly aggressive, with jokes and barbs (triggered by a "punch line," a revealing term) leveled at laughingstocks and scapegoats of all varieties. The elderly, the corpulent, the arrogant, the smitten, and the ditzy are all set up for the derisive laughter and surreptitious pleasure of audience members.

TV Violence Doesn't Explain Violence Levels

Claims that TV causes violence bear little relation to real behavior. Japanese and European kids behold media as graphically brutal as that which appears on American screens, but seventeen-year-olds in those countries commit murder at rates lower than those of American seventy-year-olds.

Likewise, youths in different parts of the United States are exposed to the same media but display drastically different violence levels. TV violence does not account for the fact that the murder rate among black teens in Washington, D.C., is twenty-five times higher than that of white teens living a few Metro stops away. It doesn't explain why, nationally, murder doubled among nonwhite and Latino youth over the last decade, but declined among white Anglo teens. Furthermore, contrary to the TV brainwashing theory, Anglo sixteen-year-olds have lower violent-crime rates than black sixty-year-olds, Latino forty-year-olds, and Anglo thirty-year-olds.

Mike Males, *Progressive*, October 1997.

The next reservation about television violence counts, a more challenging consideration, regards their implication that television violence has a direct relationship to the outbreak of violence in the real world. Such a connection is not an element in this particular type of research because no data pertaining to this relationship have been gathered. In disregard of this limitation, the authors of the 1995 cable-funded University of California at Santa Barbara (UCSB) violence count insisted that "exposure to televised violence contributes to a range of antisocial or harmful effects on many viewers." Because they had not conducted any research of their own on this matter, this error is sufficient to erode credibility in the quantitative work that was actually done.

The Difference Between TV and Real-World Violence

Television violence counts are frequently allowed to imply real-world violent effects because the word "violence" is used in both contexts and would seem to imply a semantic equivalency. Television violence and real-world violence, however, are not at all equivalent. Murder is a frequent crime on television but a rare crime in real life; slayer and victim are strangers on television but friends or family members in the real world. According to one study, (a) in the real world half of all murder victims are black, but on television only 7.3% are black, and (b) half of those arrested for serious crimes in the United States are black, but only 10% arrested on TV are black. John Fiske and John Hartley concluded, "It would appear that television violence is not the same as real violence." There is little chance they would be the same because the televised version is devoted to unworldly ends, in wholehearted service to dramatic conventions. Television violence must occur after well-plotted intimations, it must be reasonably sanitary, and it must be thoroughly redressed and concluded at the close, with no lingering, unnerving aftereffects; in these particulars, it is far removed from common brutalities in everyday life.

The third reservation regarding violence counts expands on the second: There exists a fallacious underpinning to all violence counts that calls into question their relevancy in any way to the issue of televised violence and its effects. These studies' simplicity, which would seem to be their strength, may be their undoing. This literature can account for what is sent via television, but by its very nature it has nothing to contribute to an understanding of what is received by viewers and how it is processed. The condition of reception—

about which violence counts research has nothing to say and can have nothing to say—is the central question in the television violence controversy and cannot lie concealed and unaddressed. In fact, there is ample evidence that the material sent is not at all the same as the material received—that each viewer ignores, selects, interprets, and misinterprets the content according to his or her needs and temperament at the moment. British scholar Barrie Gunter summarizes,

> In the effects research literature, it has become clear from behavioral, emotional, and perceptual measures of viewers' reactions to media content that the audience can be highly discriminating about violent portrayals and that unitary definitions of violence are relatively meaningless.

Even very young children are highly discrete and self-serving users of media violence. In short, reception is all, and violence counts reveal nothing about this.

Finally, the very act of counting violent incidents on television, an act that would seem to be unvarnished, is layered with unexpressed assumptions. People do not count things that are not of concern. Deciding to count these particular items is tantamount to labeling them problematic. Thus, even before an enumeration begins, its objects may be conceived of as rank, like cases of tuberculosis. There is an accusatory thrust to the acts of data collection and their public dissemination when there should not be ideally. Violence count researchers have managed in a clandestine fashion, and with the careless connivance of all involved, to have fashioned a "social problem," one whose existence or lack of existence demands much more deliberate thought.

This discussion of what should be the least convoluted treatment of television violence—the simple count of violent incidents—has unexpectedly brought us directly into the complexities of the matter. What exactly is being sent? More significantly, what exactly is being received and to what effect? . . .

The Response to Violent Content

Although the total volume of violent entertainment on television has to all appearances been consistently steady throughout the years, the critical response to the content has been consistently cyclic. Concern has flared and subsided, only to flare and subside again. As one measure of the nation's alternately increasing and decreasing apprehension, the number of citations to articles discussing television violence from 1950 to the present was determined in a magazine index (*Reader's Guide to Periodical Literature*) and a newspaper index (*New York Times*). It was found that there have been six peaks of high numbers of articles regarding television violence (1964, 1969, 1972, 1977, 1981, and 1994) alternating with periods when very few were published. On average, 6 years passed between peaks. Assuming that magazine and newspaper editors have a well-developed sense of the interests of their readers or they would not occupy the positions they do for long, these peaks in article numbers can be taken as an indicator of peaks in public concern regarding television violence. . . .

The existence of this repeated cycle of ferocious concern and then apathy is telling in its own right. The matter has never been laid to rest, nor is it ever likely to be. Each convulsion of public debate predicts the exhausted lull that will follow and sets the stage for the next round, several years later, of rhetorical frenzy. One reason the debate cannot be settled may be the vocabulary by which it is conducted. The words used to describe television are often polarizing terms that defeat clear thought. Television is a "vast wasteland," the "boob tube" that delivers "eye candy," content of "the lowest common denominator," to "couch potatoes." Striking preemptively, this arsenal of derogatory terms can obliterate the phenomenon than needs to be understood and remove it from any possibility of understanding. This vocabulary, useful for combative purposes but useless for intelligent comprehension, suggests a grander reason that the issue of television violence can never be settled for good. To all appearances, no one truly wants to conclude the debate. Cynthia Cooper refers to "years of repetitive inquiry with very few results." The matter must have a certain utility, one waiting to be detailed, that sustains its survival.

The recurrence of the social issue of television violence is analogous to the recurrence of the individual's daily viewing of some version of video violence. Just as, in the large, social forces on a regular basis like to have a go at television violence, so too in the small does each viewer take in a frequent dose of television violence, whether that symbolic aggression comes in a blatant form (an action-adventure movie or an MTV video) or in a cleverly disguised one (such as a situation comedy or a golf match). The need for society to launch periodic attacks on television violence mimics the need for individuals to aggress within the permissible domain of television violence. . . .

Although the historical continuities in violent entertainment offerings are important, as are the continuities in censorious criticism, most important are the continuities in spectating. People have liked, and continue to like, observing violent spectacles. James Twitchell factually notes, "We have craved violent spectacle whether it was carved on cave walls, engraved on Persian tablets, enacted in Roman coliseums, or imaged in pixels on illuminated screens." In this regard, television would seem to be providing updated and streamlined content for an age-old human proclivity. This service may account in part for the medium's popularity: Americans on average spend 80% of their total media time with television.

Several provisional statements regarding the viewing of television violence are offered here. First, watching this content is an entirely voluntary behavior. Virtually no one is compelled to observe this order of content; even toddlers, chancing on material too explosive, will exercise discretion by leaving the room or trying to change the channel. (This essential stipulation of voluntariness is violated in every laboratory study on the topic.) Second, the voluntary viewer knows that the content is symbolic and is not live. If the spectator does not perceive the content as symbols at a distance, it will soon produce a contrary and unwanted effect, and the spectator is likely to defect, which neither the broadcaster nor the spectator desires. Third, the voluntary spectator views the violent entertainment in a relaxed, nondidactic frame of mind. The spectator is actively seeking release and not instruction. Television viewing is mainly the occasion for discharge, not absorption. Every viewer knows this, but every social critic, spine stiffened, forgets this fact. Voluntary, symbol seeking, and relaxing are features of television violence spectating. They are set as a challenge to the frequent misconstruction of television viewing as an inflicted, passive, and possibly overstimulating activity.

> *"It is the opinion of major experts in this area, . . . based on extensive research, that violent video games are harmful to children."*

Violent Video Games Encourage Violent Behavior

Dave Grossman

In the following viewpoint, originally delivered as a statement before the New York State legislature, Dave Grossman, a retired lieutenant colonel in the U.S. Army, argues that violent video games are harmful to children because they teach them how to aim and shoot guns. According to Grossman, Michael Carneal, a teenager unfamiliar with real guns, fired eight shots and made eight hits on students at his high school, a feat expert marksmen could not reproduce. Grossman claims that Carneal mastered his skills playing first-person shooter video games. Unfortunately, Grossman contends, the video game industry deliberately markets these "murder simulators" to children.

As you read, consider the following questions:

1. In Grossman's opinion, how do video game shooters differ from traditional marksmen?
2. Why does the author believe that the video game industry should be regulated like the alcohol and tobacco industries?
3. According to Grossman, what criteria must video game makers meet to be held legally liable to murdered victims' families?

Dave Grossman, statement before the New York State Legislature, October 1999.

I am Lieutenant Colonel Dave Grossman, U.S. Army, (Retired). My expertise in the area of human aggression and violence includes service as a West Point psychology professor, a professor of military science, the author of a Pulitzer nominated book and numerous peer reviewed encyclopedia entries on this topic. . . .

It is my professional opinion, and it is the opinion of major experts in this area (such as the American Medical Association [AMA], the American Psychiatric Association [APA], the National Institute of Mental Health [NIMH], the American Academy of Mental Health, and the Surgeon General), based on extensive research, that violent video games are harmful to children. Legislation to rate these games, and enforcement of the ratings in order to keep the violent games out of the hands of children, is essential to the safety and security of the population of New York. The games that permit a child to hold and aim a gun, and fire it at humans, are particularly harmful, since these devices teach shooting skills. They are firearms training devices at best, and murder simulators at worst. . . .

A Case Study

The classic case of the influence of video games can be found in the Paducah, Kentucky, school shooting [on December 1, 1997]. I served as a consultant in this case, and my understanding of the facts, based upon official records, is that. . . Michael Carneal, a 14-year-old boy who had never fired a handgun before, stole a pistol, fired a few practice shots the night before and came into his school the next morning with the gun. In this case 8 shots were apparently fired, for 8 hits—4 of them head shots, one neck, and 3 upper torso. This is simply astounding, unprecedented marksmanship, especially when it comes from a child who apparently had never fired a real pistol in his life (prior to stealing the gun) and had only fired a .22 caliber rifle once at a summer camp.

I am an Army Ranger, "expert" qualified on all major U.S. small arms and many North Atlantic Treaty Organization (NATO) weapons, an instructor for the American Society of Law Enforcement Trainers (ASLET); the International Association Society of Law Enforcement Firearms Instructors

(IALEFI); the Bureau of Alcohol, Tobacco and Firearms Emergency Response Teams; the California Highway Patrol Academy; and numerous other state patrol academies. I have fired many tens of thousands of rounds of ammunition, and even with all of this I sincerely doubt that I could have fired as accurately under these circumstances. Indeed, I have never heard of anything remotely like this in its degree of deadly accuracy under these circumstances. The Illinois Highway Patrol in an assessment of the accuracy of their officers across several years found that the average officer, in the average engagement, at the average distance of 23 feet, hit with 13% of the rounds fired. In the Amadu Dialo shooting in New York City [on February 4, 1999], four members of an elite NYPD unit fired 41 rounds at an unarmed African immigrant, at point-blank range, and hit 19 times. That is the norm, even in the best of conditions, among trained, professional law enforcement officers. In [the August 10, 1999], Jewish daycare center shootings in Los Angeles, the shooter is reported to have fired 70 shots, and wounded 5 individuals. This is what should be expected from an untrained shooter.

I trained a battalion of Green Berets, the Texas Rangers, the California Highway Patrol, the Australian Federal Police, and numerous other elite military and law enforcement organizations, and when I told them of Michael Carneal's achievement they were simply amazed. Nowhere in the annals of military or law enforcement or criminal history can any of us find an equivalent achievement, and this from a 14-year-old boy with no previous experience in firing a handgun. Michael Carneal had never fired an actual pistol before, but he had fired thousands of bullets in the video game "murder simulators." His superhuman accuracy, combined with the fact that he "stood still," firing two-handed, not wavering far to the left or far to the right in his shooting "field," and firing only one shot at each target, are all behaviors that are completely unnatural to either trained or "native" shooters, behaviors that could only have been learned in a video game.

It is not natural to fire one shot at every target. The normal, near universal response of anyone with a semiautomatic weapon, in combat or while hunting, is to fire at a target until it drops, and then to move on to another target. But, if you are very, very good at video games, you will only fire one shot at every target, not even waiting for that target to drop before moving on to another target, because you "know" (from countless thousands of previous repetitions of the action) that you have hit and you "know" that the target will fall when it is hit with no need to waste time shooting it further. (Some games do not use the one-shot-one-kill model, but many, if not most, do.)

The World of the First-Person Shooter

The world of video games is Darwinian, paranoid and controlled. There is no empathy. Studies have shown that kids who play video games contribute less to classroom charities. There is no altruism in *Twisted Metal* or *Resident Evil*. You only win by killing. Is it any wonder that the military use these games to simulate combat. Video gaming requires a Zen-like approach: One shot per kill; no time to celebrate a score or curse a miss. You have to go on the next obliteration. This just serves to desensitize the, often, first-person shooter.

Michael Brody, *The Brown University Child and Adolescent Behavior Letter*, November 2000.

As a player in the video game your goal is simply to rack up the highest "score" as quickly as possible. And, many of the video games (such as "House of the Dead," "Goldeneye," or "Turok") give bonus effects for head shots. This is reinforced by Michael Carneal's "blank and passive" facial expression, and his report that it was all "like a dream" which are common reactions of someone who is in the "flow state" associated with completing an operantly conditioned response under a stressful situation: like children in a fire drill, or an expert typist finding the next key. These kind of video games provide the "motor reflexes" responsible for over 75% of the firing on the modern battlefield. In addition, they provide violent suggestions and reinforcement for violent behavior. . . .

I have reviewed these conclusions with other experts in the field of law enforcement marksmanship training. Based upon my communications with them, the heads of the three major national and international law enforcement training organizations (IALEFI, ASLET and PPCT [Pressure Point Control Tactics Management Systems Inc.]) have all concurred with these conclusions, and they have told me that they would be willing to serve (pro bono) as expert witnesses in a lawsuit against the manufacturers of these games. Certainly, if the information I received is correct, no firearms expert can deny the extraordinary marksmanship achievement in the Michael Carneal case (and many others like it), and that the influence of video games is the only possible explanation for that aspect of this tragedy.

The Case Against Video Games

Based upon research outlined in my book, *On Killing*, President Bill Clinton stated in his national radio address on April 24, 1999, following the Littleton, Colorado, shootings [at Columbine High School on April 20, 1999] that: "A former Lieutenant Colonel and psychologist, Professor David Grossman, has said that these games teach young people to kill with all the precision of a military training program, but none of the character training that goes along with it. For children who get the right training at home and who have the ability to distinguish between real and unreal consequences, they're still games. But for children who are especially vulnerable to the lure of violence, they can be far more." The President's conclusions are completely correct. The U.S. Army has taken the basic Super Nintendo, replaced the plastic pistol with a plastic M-16, modified the targets that appear on the screen, and this device (known as the Multipurpose Arcade Combat Simulator [MACS]) is used extensively for military marksmanship training. Similarly, the U.S. Marine Corps has licensed the basic "first person shooter" game "Doom," and is using it to train their combat fire teams in tactics and to rehearse (or "script") combat actions of killing. (Some claim that the Marines only use it to develop teamwork, but if that was the desire they could use flag football; the Marines' goal is to develop teamwork in killing.

The video game industry cannot market these devices to the military to train individuals whose job it is to kill, and then claim that they have no expectation that such devices would be potentially harmful when marketed to children. The video game industry blatantly markets their products as killing devices.

Marketing Murder

One advertisement, in a "gaming" magazine, for a joystick that gives feedback (thus you feel the recoil of a gun when you pull the trigger), says: "Psychiatrists say it is important to feel something when you kill."

1. An ad for one video game says: "Kill your friends guilt free."
2. Another ad for a home video game shooting system says: "More fun than shooting your neighbor's cat."
3. Recent ads for "Quake II" (a follow-on to "Doom," by the same manufacturer) says: "We took what was killer, and made it mass murder."
4. An ad for the same game has a picture of a corpse with a toe tag, saying: "He practiced on a PC." (Personal computer.)
5. An ad for a Sony Playstation controller that gives feedback shows an old man and his wife, saying: "George Anderson, 64. Responsible for thousands of deaths and ruthless beatings, is about to discover how it feels."
6. An ad for one Playstation game says: "Destroying your enemies is not enough . . . you must devour their souls."
7. An ad for a networking kit says: "Gratuitous violence is 200 times faster with a D-Link Network."

Thus, the industry's own ads acknowledge that their products are "killer . . . mass murder . . . ruthless beatings . . . [and] gratuitous beatings." The industry's own rating systems indicate that many of their games are inappropriate for children. Yet the industry has spent enormous sums of money fighting legislative initiatives designed to regulate the availability of their products to children. Imagine if the gun, tobacco, alcohol, or even the fireworks industry had rated and acknowledged their products as harmful to children, but then refused to accept regulation of the sale of their products to children. Furthermore, imagine if these industries had intentionally and irresponsibly marketed their products with advertisements clearly oriented toward children. If this were the situation, then these industries would arguably find themselves subject to even greater litigation and liability than is currently the case.

In one case, the book *Hit Man*, was used as a manual to commit a multiple murder. The family of the victims of this murder sued the publisher and author of this book. Based on my reading of the decision in that case (which was upheld by the U.S. Supreme Court), this case could be brought to trial because the book, *Hit Man*, taught criminal behavior, exhorted the reader to engage in criminal behavior, and then taught the reader to develop a blatant disregard for human life.

It is interesting to me to apply these same criteria to the video games. The violent video games teach criminal behavior: i.e., shooting human beings, to include motor skills, aiming skills, target selection, and trigger control.

The video games and their advertisements exhort the reader to engage in criminal behavior while teaching blatant disregard for human life: being rewarded for harming and killing humans, and: "Kill your friends. . . . More fun than shooting your neighbor's cat. . . . Destroying your enemies is not enough . . . you must devour their souls."

The video game industry knows that their products are not for children, and they openly support and expect enforcement of the ratings on their products. In a current issue of *PC Gamer Magazine* (the industry's leading magazine), the game "Kingpin" is discussed. (This is a hyperviolent game in which the player leads a life of crime, killing, pimping and selling drugs, working up to a position of leadership.)

There are certain people who believe "Kingpin" crosses the line of good taste and shouldn't be in the hands of children or young teens. Those people would be absolutely right! If you see the game in the store, you'll notice a big yellow sticker across the front of the box stating the game was designed for mature audiences, and that you'll need an ID to prove you're old enough to buy it.

Who Should Enforce Ratings?

In other words, it is the responsibility of stores and society to enforce the industry's rating system. And they are right. In that same magazine there is a review of a new, hyperviolent game called "Soldier of Fortune," in which the magazine says:

> Don't expect to be able to buy this one without a picture ID . . . It is inevitable that, given the recent controversy regarding violence in games, "Soldier of Fortune" will attract its share of flack . . . Raven is hoping to head at least some of the criticism off with . . . warnings on the packaging. 'Raven's plan from day one was to make a game for mature audiences that would carry a mature ESBR rating,' says [the manufacturer]. 'When the rating has been established . . . how can they criticize the game? If people don't take advantage of the tools we are providing, they're the ones opening themselves up to criticism.'

In other words, again, according to the industry, they are counting on us to enforce the ratings. If we do not enforce their ratings, we are to blame. And they are right. . . . They will claim that their rating and labeling system is enough to protect kids from the products that they themselves admit should not be in the hands of children, and they will oppose enforcement of their warning labels. This is simply offensive to the intelligence of the legislators and people of the great state of New York. Again, what would happen if the gun or tobacco or alcohol industry had tried to use that logic?

"*There is not a shred of evidence in the academic literature to support the allegation that a violent video game leads to aggressive behavior in real life.*"

Violent Video Games Do Not Encourage Violent Behavior

Douglas Lowenstein

The research methods used by many studies of violent video games are flawed, claims Douglas Lowenstein in the following viewpoint, originally given as congressional testimony before the Senate Committee on Commerce. For example, he argues, some studies define violence as "the intentional injury of another person," but it is illogical to compare vaporizing animated characters to the intentional killing of a real human being. According to Lowenstein, unbiased studies reviewing the research have concluded that there is no link between violent video games and aggressive behavior. Lowenstein is president of the Interactive Digital Software Association.

As you read, consider the following questions:
1. According to Lowenstein, why does the Australian study he cites stand out above all others?
2. In the author's opinion, what is the flaw in the way video game research is carried out?
3. How do television and video games differ, in Lowenstein's opinion?

Douglas Lowenstein, testimony before the Senate Committee on Commerce on the Effects of Interactive Violence on Children, March 21, 2000.

This testimony is submitted on behalf of the Interactive Digital Software Association (IDSA) the trade body representing U.S. video and computer game software companies that publish games for use in the home. In 1999, the industry generated $6.1 billion in retail software sales. IDSA's 32 members account for 90% of the edutainment and entertainment software sold in the U.S. . . .

I certainly understand the interest in [the effects of interactive violence on children] in the aftermath of tragic school shootings between 1996 and 2000, as well as the frenzied media reports—often inaccurate and misleading—about interactive entertainment in the months after the shooting in Littleton, Colorado. This is an important topic which deserves a fair and balanced discussion.

By far the most exhaustive and objective analysis of this subject was released in December 1999 by the Government of Australia in a study entitled "Computer Games and Australians Today." This detailed report . . . stands out above all others for two reasons: first, it was carried out by a government with a history of tough regulation of entertainment content for the purpose of determining whether government regulation is merited; second, unlike some of those who will appear before you today, it was written by authors who lack preconceived points of view on the issue of whether violent games lead to aggressive behavior. I think it is especially helpful to the Senate Commerce, Science, and Transportation Committee since it provides an independent, unbiased, peer-based evaluation of some of the research you will hear about today. . . . Let me quote to you here the key conclusion.

> "The accumulating evidence—provided largely by researchers keen to demonstrate the games' undesirable effects—does indicate that *it is very hard to find such effects and that they are unlikely to be substantial* (emphasis added)." . . .

The Research on Interactive Entertainment

The Australian study updated a 1995 study conducted by Kevin Durkin, Ph.D., Associate Professor of Psychology, University of Western Australia. In that study, which reviewed all literature on the effects of video games on users, Durkin concluded, "Overall, evidence is limited, but so far does not lend strong support to the claims that computer games play promotes aggressive behavior."

As noted earlier, the new study reaches much the same conclusion after evaluating research carried out since the 1995 study was published.

A few key points from the Australia study are worth reporting. First, government researchers found in a national survey that "most people associate positive feelings such as enjoyment, happiness, exhilaration, relaxation, and challenge with playing computer games": and that "young players report that aggressive content is not the central attraction of games. Many players said that they perceive the aggressive content as fantastic and preposterous, with the result that they do not take it seriously; they do not perceive their own actions as harming others since they do not believe the characters are real or suffer pain." This punctures the oft-repeated statement that kids prefer violent games or that they take them seriously.

I want to cite briefly a few important studies covered by the Australians. Derek Scott, as reported in the *Journal of Psychology*, had hypothesized that the more aggressive games subjects played, the more aggressive they would become. He set out to prove this point of view, and failed. In fact, Scott found that the moderately aggressive games substantially *decreased* feelings of aggression, whereas the highly aggressive game resulted in no more of an increase in aggression than the nonaggressive game. "Results are discussed in terms of a general lack of support for the commonly held view that playing aggressive computer games causes an individual to feel more aggressive" Scott wrote. There are several other studies which have sought to prove that the more aggressive the game played, the more significant the impact on behavior, and they have not been able to demonstrate this link, suggesting that there is not a nexus between the level of aggression in a game and behavior outside it.

The Australian authors also note a 1997 study by Dutch researchers E.G.M. Van Schie and O. Wiegman who believed that the more users were exposed to violent games, the more aggressively they would behave. In fact, they reported, no relationship was found between the amount of play and aggressiveness.

In sum, the Australian Government study concludes that, "Despite several attempts to find effects of aggressive content in either experimental studies or field studies, at best only weak and ambiguous evidence has emerged."

Examining the Research Methodology

In evaluating any research on this topic, pro or con, it is important to carefully evaluate the methodology, definitions, and interpretation of the data. In this regard, Dr. Jeffrey Goldstein notes: "Neither the quantity nor the quality of research on video games does much to inspire confidence in solid conclusions about their effects. Nearly every study suffers from vague definitions (of violence or aggression), ambiguous measurements (confusing aggressive play with aggressive behavior), questionable measures of aggression (such as blasts of noise or self-reports of prior aggression), or overgeneralizations of the data."

Take, for example, the issue of how aggression is defined in the studies. Psychologists define violence or aggression as "the intentional injury of another person." Yet, in video games, there is neither intent to injure nor a living victim. Nonetheless, some researchers loosely claim that the goal of certain games is to " kill" opponents. But there is no literal killing and it is a massive leap of logic to suggest that vaporizing an animated character leads to or causes real world killing.

Another flaw in some research on this topic lies in how the research is carried out. Many of them, for example, are conducted in lab settings which do not replicate even remotely the environment and experience of those who play games for entertainment.

Dr. Goldstein writes: "Experiments that claim to study the effects of playing electronic games rarely study play at all. In reality, a game player chooses when and what to play, and enters in a different frame of mind than someone who is required to 'play' on demand. Some have argued that the link between media violence and aggressive behavior is as strong as the link between cigarette smoking and cancer. This is not so. We can measure the presence or absence of disease with reasonable precision, but we cannot easily or reliably measure aggressive behavior in laboratory settings. We have only indirect and often questionable measures of aggression at our disposal."

Refuting the Claims Against Video Games

It is true that some research claims that video games lead to aggressive behavior in the real world. But often these are conclusions and speculation not supported by the underlying research. It is argued, for example, that video games reinforce murderous behavior! Last time I checked, murder was the taking of a human being's life. Equating that to shooting alien creatures is totally unsubstantiated, and requires one to assume that the player will believe that what is permitted in the fantasy world he or she voluntarily entered is sanctioned in real life.

Video Gamers Are Not Homicidal Maniacs

Simulated combat has always been part of children's play, and violence is an integral aspect of many venerable genres, including not only horror and war stories but the western, the spy thriller, and the murder mystery. Doom is one of the most popular computer games ever, played by millions of teenagers and adults across the country. They are not, for the most part, homicidal maniacs.

And that, in a nutshell, is the problem with blaming violence in popular culture for violence in real life. Everyone is exposed to the influences, . . . yet virtually no one commits mass murder. Is it possible that, generally speaking, our moral values do not come from video games and action movies?

Jacob Sullum, *Reason*, May 19, 1999.

In fact, rather than suggesting that playing violent games leads to aggressive behavior in the real world, at best there is some weak evidence that this activity may lead to more aggressive play. In 1999, British researcher Mark Griffiths reviewed the literature on the subject and noted that what some researchers report as aggressive behavior is really only an increase in aggressive play—such as mock battles or running around making believe you're killing aliens—with no intent to injure, as required by the standard psychological definition of aggression. This point cannot be overemphasized. There is a world of difference between running around making believe you're killing aliens, or martial arts play fighting, and picking up a real weapon and shooting your friends. *There is not a shred of evidence in the academic literature to support the allegation that a violent video game leads to aggressive behavior in real life.*

Some researchers do claim that they have established a link between playing a violent game and aggressive behavior, such as Craig A. Anderson and Karen E. Dill. But their measure of aggressive behavior is not evidence of an actual violent act or the actual intent to injure someone, but the intensity and duration of noise blasts initiated by their subjects. I am not a psychologist but I would suggest that basing a conclusion that violent games lead to aggressive behavior on how loud and long someone blows a horn is not a sound basis for policy or pronouncements. Another measure used in this research is reaction time to aggressive words flashed on a screen after playing a violent game. A faster response was presumed to indicate aggressive thoughts. But it means nothing of the sort, anymore than if one played a golf game and then responded faster to the word "putter" means that you have golf on the brain. This kind of weak data represents the high water mark for research seeking to establish that violent video games lead to aggressive behavior, and it is extremely weak and ambiguous at best, and is contradicted by other research.

Looking at Video Game Players

Yet another weakness in some of the research is that it fails to control for the pre-existing tendencies that subjects bring into the research. Griffiths points out that more aggressive children may be drawn to more violent games. And the Australian authors suggest that "it would appear plausible that the direction of effect is from player to game. Computer games cannot turn players into boys. A more reasonable interpretation is that people with certain characteristics seek out certain types of games. It remains uncertain whether involvement in aggressive games by already aggressive individuals contributes to the exacerbation of their aggressive tendencies, provides a harmless avenue for its discharge, or makes no difference."

Another statement often made about video games is that one can extrapolate the effects of television research to computer games. This is not only bad science, it may be wildly misleading. One difference between video games and TV is that video game players exert control over what takes place on the screen. They are participants in an interactive system that allows them to regulate the pace and character of the game. This, in turn, gives them increased control over their own emotional states during play. A substantial body of research demonstrates that perceived control over events reduces their emotional or stressful impact.

In 1999 and 2000, much attention has been paid in Congress and the media to claims that the military's use of video game technology in training suggests that these games when used in the home train kids to kill. There is no evidence to support this wild claim, the purveyor of it has absolutely no research on which the claim is based, and the Pentagon itself dismisses the notion that it uses simulators to teach soldiers to kill. I will not dwell on this issue here, but will be happy to provide detail on this claim should the Committee desire.

Taking Proactive Steps

Does this mean we do nothing? The answer is no. In the spring of 1999, I testified before this Committee and pledged to take a series of steps to address concerns about violent video games, including stepping up promotion of the Entertainment Software Rating Board (ESRB) working with retailers to uphold the ratings at the point of sale, and addressing concerns about video game advertising. We have redeemed all of these pledged.

Our industry has been and continues to be extremely proactive in addressing concerns about the content of the small minority of products which give rise to the concerns covered in this hearing. We agree that some games are not appropriate for young children. That's precisely what the ESRB ratings tell consumers. The single most meaningful step industry and government can take to protect children from games that may not be appropriate for them is to educate parents about how to use ESRB ratings.

To that end, the ESRB mounted a major campaign during the 1999 holiday season to raise awareness and use of its ratings. This campaign included paid ads in national publications with significant parent readership. It also included a PSA featuring golf superstar Tiger Woods encouraging parents to "Check the Ratings" before buying games for their kids. ESRB also reached out to various national groups such as the PTA, Mothers Against Violence in America, and the YMCA and YWCA to distribute information about ESRB ratings to their constituents.

Informing the Public

Another major element of the effort was to encourage retailers to carry information about ESRB ratings in their stores, and to adopt policies to uphold the ratings at the point of sale by not selling Mature or Adult Only games to persons under 17. Such national chains as Toys "R" Us, Babbages, Electronics Boutique, and Funcoland all agreed to either actively restrict sales of "M" rated games to persons under 17 or to use their best efforts to prevent such sales. In addition, the ESRB printed and distributed over 5 million brochures on how to use ESRB ratings to retailers.

Separately, the three major video game console hardware companies—Nintendo, Sega, and Sony—all agreed in the fall of 1999 to include in their hardware packages information on the ESRB, a step which put critical ratings information into the hands of millions of new consumers this holiday season.

IDSA was active in other areas as well. In the fall of 1999, our Board of Directors created a new Advertising Review Council (ARC) within the independent ESRB organization to develop and enforce an expanded advertising Code which for the first time includes content standards and various restrictions on the placement of ads for video and PC games. The new ARC opened its doors for business February 1, 2000. The ARC has secured support for its content guidelines from the three major video game magazine chains who have agreed to adopt the ARC code as their internal standards and practices.

We're also pleased that the ESRB reached an agreement late in 1999 with AOL in which AOL will adopt the ESRB ratings on its game service, a major step toward expanding ESRB's Internet presence.

We also welcome the study by the Surgeon General of the United States into the causes of youth violence, and will cooperate with that office as it proceeds.

Late in 1999, the IDSA conducted research asking parents who is responsible for controlling the video games children play. The overwhelming majority of respondents said it is up to the parents. Our industry will continue to make products that appeal to people of all tastes and interests. Some of these will not be appropriate for younger consumers. But absent unconstitutional restrictions on content, and absent any compelling scientific research showing that playing violent games is harmful, the best way to ensure that kids don't play games that are not suitable for them is to maximize parental awareness and use of the existing rating system. Our industry pledges to you that we will continue to actively promote the ESRB system to increase its utilization by parents, and we hope you and others who share your concerns will join us in that ongoing campaign.

While the subject of this hearing is the effects of violent interactive games on children, I want to briefly point out that there is a growing body of evidence that video games have many positive effects on players, including enhancing educational performance, improving spatial skills, improving cognitive development, and as therapeutic tools to treat attention deficit disorders, among other things. I hope we can address these benefits at some future hearing rather than continually and exclusively focusing on the issue of violence. . . .

There is no compelling research which supports the belief that playing violent video games in the real world causes aggressive behavior in the real world. Put another way, there is no scientific basis to argue that entering the fantasy world of Doom in the home using a mouse causes players to gun down their friends in the school yard.

But even if one were to agree with those who believe there is cause for concern about the effects of violent entertainment on children, the question is what can be done about it? Video games and computer games are protected forms of expression under our Constitution. Some may not like particular games, but the case law is clear that efforts by government to regulate violent content is unconstitutional.

"There is a sound basis for concluding that some popular music can help lead some young people to violence."

Rap Music Leads to Youth Violence

Thomas L. Jipping

Thomas L. Jipping maintains in the following viewpoint that the parallel between musician Marilyn Manson's lyrics—which often discuss murderous revenge against bullies—and the motives of teen killers who listen to Manson is no coincidence. According to Jipping, studies show that consumers who listen to music with such harmful themes exhibit antisocial behavior because young people often internalize negative messages. He claims that heavy metal rock and gangsta rap glamorize violence, rape, and murder, and could be harmful to vulnerable young people. Jipping is author of *Heavy Metal, Rap, and America's Youth: Issues and Alternatives.*

As you read, consider the following questions:

1. How does Jipping link media-violence research and research on the impact of music?
2. What research does the author cite to support his argument that for young people music is more powerful than television?
3. What two conclusions does Jipping claim are inescapable regarding the destructive themes of rock and rap music?

On April 20, 1999, two teenagers killed 12 of their peers, a teacher, and themselves at Columbine High School in Littleton, Colorado. A few days later, Colorado Governor Bill Owens warned in a radio address of a "virus loose within our culture." This virus is a mutated and resistant strain of the same contagion this author wrote about seven years ago in the pages of *The World & I*. Some popular music is part of this cultural virus, which can help lead some young people to violence.

Five days after the massacre, Tim Russert, host of NBC's *Meet the Press*, reported on the show that the Littleton killers idolized shock-rocker Marilyn Manson, described even by the music press as an "ultra-violent satanic rock monstrosity." Other teenage killers have done the same. These include Kip Kinkel, who murdered his parents and two students at Thurston High School in Springfield, Oregon; Andrew Wurst, who killed a teacher at an eighth-grade dance in Edinboro, Pennsylvania; and Luke Woodham, who murdered his parents and a classmate in Pearl, Mississippi.

The pattern was the same as other violent youths whose plans were foiled. A Leesburg, Virginia, teenager suspended for threatening students who made fun of his literary work was fascinated with Marilyn Manson. Five Wisconsin teenagers who had carefully planned a bloodbath at their school in revenge for being teased were Manson fans.

The Parallel Is No Coincidence

Dismissing all this as coincidence becomes increasingly difficult. The facts of these and other instances of youth violence parallel not just the generally violent themes but the specifically violent action in the music these boys consumed.

Manson repeatedly dwells on revenge and violence against the objects of his hatred. In "Lunchbox," he says that the next bully who "fu**s with me" is "gonna get my metal. . . . Pow pow pow." In "Irresponsible Hate Anthem," he responds to the "selective judgments" of others by saying "get your gun." In "The Beautiful People," he says there is "no time to discriminate, hate every motherfu**er that's in your way." In "Man That You Fear," he warns that "I'll make everyone pay and you will see . . . the boy that you loved is the monster you fear." And in "The Suck for Your Solution," he says that "I'm gonna hate you tomorrow because you make me hate you today."

Ordained in the Church of Satan, Manson wrote in the foreword to the book *Satan Speaks* that its late founder, Anton LaVey, "was the most righteous man I've ever known." On CNN's *The American Edge* program, Manson explained his view that "you are your own god. It's a lot about self-preservation. . . . It's the part of you that no longer has hope in mankind. And you realize that you are the only thing you believe in."

In one interview, Manson explained that when he attended a public school "they would always kick my ass. . . . So I didn't end up having a lot of friends and music was the only thing I had to enjoy. So I got into [heavy metal rock bands] Kiss, Black Sabbath and things like that."

Despite all these parallels, Manson's response to the Littleton massacre was predictable: "The media has unfairly scapegoated the music industry . . . and has speculated—with no basis in truth—that artists like myself are in some way to blame." He is wrong. There is a sound basis for concluding that some popular music can help lead some young people to violence. That conclusion rests on three pillars.

Examining the Evidence

First, as the American Medical Association (AMA) concluded in September 1996, the "link between media violence and real life violence has been proven by science time and again." Many leading medical associations, as well as commissions and task forces created to study the issue, have over the last three decades documented that, in the words of columnist William Raspberry, "television violence begets real-world violence."

Professor Leonard Eron concluded in a speech at the Harvard University School of Public Health that literally hundreds of studies provide "convincing evidence that the observation of violence, as seen in standard everyday television entertainment, does affect the aggressive behavior of the viewer." One writer reported that "more than 1,000 studies since 1955 have linked media violence and aggressive behavior." A television network's own study concluded that more than one-fourth of young violent offenders had consciously imitated crime techniques learned from television.

The American people share the same conclusion. In fact, polls reveal that the percentage of Americans concerned that media violence contributes to real-life violence has grown by 50 percent during the 1990s.

Stayskal. © 1995 by Tribune Media Services, Inc. Reprinted with permission.

The most common response by the television industry is that programming merely reflects what people already wish to consume, that the medium is entirely reactive and does not itself cause anything. In addition to common sense and experience, research evidence exists that this may not be true. A group of European and American researchers, for example, found that "the data across nations support the conclusion that viewing televised violence leads to aggressive behaviour and not vice versa."

The Impact of Music

Second, music is as powerful as television in its impact on people in general.

In September 1985, Joseph Steussay, professor of music history at the University of Texas, testified in U.S. Senate hearings that "tons of research has been done on the interrelationship of music and human behavior. . . . [M]usic affects human behavior. It affects our moods, our attitudes, our emotions, and our behavior." Pharmacologist Dr. Arram Goldstein of Stanford University found that 96 percent of people got their biggest thrills from music. Researcher Anne Rosenfeld put it well, describing the power of music as "a miracle akin to that of language. . . . But music is more than a language."

Third, music is more powerful than television for young people in particular. The AMA concluded in a 1989 report that music has a greater influence than television on the lives of teenagers. Two other researchers more recently confirmed that "the average teenager listens to 10,500 hours of rock music during the years between the 7th and 12th grades, and music surpasses television as an influence in teenagers' lives." Polls show that teens consider musicians as heroes far more than even athletes and rate music ahead of religion and books as factors that greatly influence their generation.

The music industry, like the television industry, claims it merely reflects and does not influence. In a commentary written for *Billboard* magazine, Hilary Rosen, president of the Recording Industry Association of America, argues that "lyrics, in essence, exhibit the action—they don't cause it. . . . [M]usic cannot cause action." This position is as false as it is self-serving. Sheila Davis, adjunct professor of lyric writing at New York University, makes the point that songs "are more than mere mirrors of society; they are a potent force in the shaping of it. . . . [P]opular songs provide the primary 'equipment for living' for America's youth."

Disputing Music Industry Claims

Three categories of research dispute Rosen's disclaimer. First, research establishes that music affects basic attitudes and values. The author of a major book on satanism writes that "Dr. T.L. Tashjian, chair of the department of psychiatry at Mount Sinai Hospital in Philadelphia, has found significant effects of rock music on the formation of values and worldview among children."

Second, music affects behavior. Studies have found, for example, that consumers of music with harmful themes are more approving of antisocial behaviors and attitudes and that consumption "correlates with increasing discomfort in family situations, a preference for friends over family, and poor academic performance."

Third, and perhaps most disturbing, consumers of negative or destructive messages listen and internalize those messages more than consumers of more neutral messages.

One study found that "fans of rock music containing potentially negative themes (i.e., suicide, homicide, and satanic themes) were more likely to report that they knew all of the words to their favorite songs and that the lyrics were important to their experience of the music."

Professor Hannelore Wass and her colleagues similarly found that fans of heavy metal music listen more, know the words better, and actually agree with the words more than fans of general rock music. She concluded that her findings "seem to dispel the notion advanced by the recording industry that teenagers are only interested in the sound of music, don't know the lyrics, and listen strictly for fun."

Public opinion parallels the evidence about music, as it does the evidence about television. Two different 1995 surveys found that more teenagers than adults believe popular music encourages antisocial behavior. A *Newsweek* analysis said popular music lyrics contribute to the "culture of aggression."

Music's Destructive Themes

Understanding the power of music, particularly in the lives of young people, is the first step. Reviewing the messages or themes delivered by this powerful medium completes the picture. Two conclusions are inescapable regarding rock and rap music, the most popular genres of music among young people today. First, negative or destructive themes are now the rule rather than the exception. Second, some popular music actively promotes these messages.

The American Academy of Pediatrics has concluded that "rock music has undergone dramatic changes since its introduction 30 years ago and is an issue of vital interest and concern for parents and pediatricians."

While 25 percent of the top-selling recordings in 1990 were hard rock or heavy metal releases, by 1995 only 10 of the 40 most popular CDs were free of profanity or lyrics dealing with drugs, violence, and sex.

As Dr. Paul King, clinical assistant professor of child and adolescent psychiatry at the University of Tennessee, describes it: "The message of heavy metal is that there is a higher power in control of the world and that power is violence—often violence presided over by Satan."

Similarly, a definitive history of rap music says that "the so-called gangsta genre of rap" is now "the leading music genre in hip hop." Music critic Leonard Pitts describes this rap style and "the sound of unredeemed violence and unrelieved ugliness." One reviewer has called N.W.A. founding member Ice Cube's platinum 1991 album *Death Certificate* an "exercise in rap brutality." An album by the Geto Boys includes a song titled "Mind of a Lunatic" containing "elements of necrophilia, murder, and other violent acts."

Heavy metal rock music and gangsta rap not only include but actually promote negative or destructive themes. A popular women's magazine concluded that "in addition to the typical teen themes of fast cars, pretty girls and social change, many heavy metal groups dwell on topics such as Satanism, drug abuse, violence and rape." *Time* magazine says: "Rock music has become a dominant—and potentially destructive—part of teenage culture. Lyrics, album covers and music videos, particularly in the rock genre called heavy metal, romanticize bondage, sexual assaults and murder."

Celebrating Violence

Professor Carl Raschke writes: "Heavy metal does not mirror the violent so much as it artistically stylizes, aggrandizes, beautifies, weaves a spell of enchantment around what would otherwise be lesser and ordinary violent behavior. . . . Heavy metal is a true aesthetics of violence. It is a metaphysics. It is the tactic of consecrating violent terror, of divinizing it."

Gangsta rap promotes violence in the same way. One editorial writer put it this way:

"The most effective rejoinder comes from Mike Davis's

"City of Quartz," a history of Los Angeles, where gangster rap was born. "In supposedly stripping bare the reality of the streets, 'telling it like it is,'" Mr. Davis writes, "they also offer an uncritical mirror to fantasy power trips of violence, sexism and greed." Rappers, take note: The key phrase is "uncritical mirror." The music "plays" at rape and murder in a way that celebrates them.

The pattern here is obvious. Heavy metal and gangsta rap "dwell on," "romanticize," "stylize," "aggrandize," "beautify," "consecrate," and offer an "uncritical mirror" for violence. The American Academy of Pediatrics concluded that, in so doing, this music contributes to "new morbidities"—including depression, suicide, and homicide—in young people. These physicians surely were doing something more than, in Marilyn Manson's words, "unfairly scapegoat[ing] the music industry."

Similarly, the AMA warned that "the vivid depiction of drug and alcohol use, suicide, violence, demonology, sexual exploitation, racism and bigotry [in some rock music] could be harmful to some young people." The most prestigious medical society in America was after something more important than, in Rosen's words, "blaming music for society's ills."

Parents Can Take Action

A wise sage once said that everything has a frame of reference. If this discussion about popular music is framed in terms of taste, it is pointless. The evidence shows persuasively, however, that the discussion should be framed in terms of harm. This more serious perspective suggests several action steps.

First, parents must visit the record stores in their area and do three things—browse, browse, and browse. This will reveal what is for sale and that some recordings already have labels warning of explicit lyrics.

Second, parents should visit those stores again and do three things—inquire, inquire, inquire. Does the store prohibit sale of labeled recordings to minors? Labeled recordings are the audio version of *Hustler* magazine, and it makes no sense to restrict one but not the other. Parents should pressure the management to adopt such a policy, including by threatening to take their business elsewhere.

Third, concerned citizens should use their power as stockholders and consumers to pressure manufacturers to stop producing harmful cultural products. This is where the difference between taste and harm is critical.

Fourth, concerned citizens should aggressively exercise their freedom of speech and denounce harmful cultural products such as the music discussed here. Sound arguments supported with the facts could, for example, become publicized resolutions adopted by city councils, service organizations, and PTA chapters. Physicians, clinical social workers, and others with experience working directly with young people could add their voice as well.

Finally, policymakers should consider applying to recordings the same restrictions that apply to visual pornography and indecent television or radio programming. The medium transmitting the cultural damage is irrelevant; indeed, the evidence shows that music is more powerful than other media. Public policy must, of course, meet fundamental constitutional requirements. If this is an issue of harm, however, pursuing this goal in a responsible manner might be appropriate.

Marilyn Manson is simply wrong that there is "no basis in truth" for the speculation that he and similar artists contribute to youth violence. In 1956, the *New York Times* called rock music "a communicable disease." Today, some popular music remains part of the cultural virus that can lead some young people to violence. The debate is not about taste but about harm. As one writer put it:

"People consume rage as entertainment; they plunk their money down, turn up the volume, and shout themselves hoarse. They shout Public Enemy's black nationalism, Slayer's ambivalent Satanism, Living Colour's warnings of environmental disaster, Nine Inch Nails' self-laceration, Anthrax's moral dialectics, Skid Row's triumphal Machismo. For a little while, it feels like actual power—until—the music stops."

Or until the killing starts.

> "*Research, although addressing many of the issues surrounding rap music, does not consistently show that it influences attitudes and behaviors.*"

Studies Have Not Established a Link Between Rap Music and Youth Violence

Becky L. Tatum

Research shows no link between rap lyrics and criminal behavior, argues Becky L. Tatum in the following viewpoint. Tatum maintains that arguments against rap are based on societal prejudices against African Americans, the primary consumers of rap music. She contends that current research on the effects of rap music has significant limitations and claims that more studies need to be conducted before any definitive conclusions can be drawn. Tatum is a criminal justice professor at Georgia State University.

As you read, consider the following questions:
1. In Tatum's opinion, what are the similarities and differences between hard core rap and heavy metal?
2. What does Tatum say are three arguments used to encourage the censorship of heavy metal and rap music?
3. What did K. Took and D. Weiss conclude about the correlation between music preferences and behavioral problems?

P opular music has traditionally been perceived as having a negative influence on adolescent youths. Criticisms of early jazz, the blues, rock n' roll, R&B and rap have all suggested that the lyrics cause youths to display negative attitudes and to engage in delinquent and antisocial behaviors. Of the contemporary music genres, rap music—in particular gangsta rap—is seen as being the most harmful to youths, and as a result, has been subjected to the harshest censorship. For example, rap is the only music genre to have a recording (*As Nasty As They Wanna Be*) to be declared 'as criminally obscene' by a federal judge or to have a recording (*Cop Killer*) boycotted by the law enforcement community. Moreover, in 1994, the negative effects of rap music were the primary focus of a congressional hearing on the violent and demeaning imagery in popular music held by the Senate Judiciary Subcommittee on Juvenile Justice.

Despite public discourse, the effects of rap music on attitudes and behaviors remain unclear, and in terms of empirical study, largely unexplored. . . .

A Historical Background

Before examining linkages between rap music and criminal and violent behavior among youths, it is important to place the music genre within a historical frame of reference. As an art form, rap music is primarily grounded in the African and African American culture. Oral language set against a musical background dates back to early African societies who used the tradition to entertain and educate audiences in tribal history and current events. In American society, rap can be found in early versions of jazz and R&B music and has traditionally been a form of verbal contest among inner city African American dwellers.

Modern rap music originated in the late 1970s in lower-class neighborhoods of New York City. Focusing on the contemporary African American urban experience, modern rap emerged as a form of cultural resistance and social protest of African American youths to their deteriorating economic and social condition. Although original songs were about partying and having a 'good time,' themes quickly evolved to include issues such as racism, police brutality, drug addiction, stereotyped racial roles and material deprivation. In short, rap music is a component of the hip hop culture; that is, the attitudes, dress, music and dance of youths residing in post-industrial inner cities. The music, in particular, represents a form of storytelling that articulates social and cultural experiences.

Although rap music is considered to be the voice of the urban African American youth, it is important to recognize the role (albeit smaller) of youths of other racial minorities, especially Puerto Rican youths, in the initiation and creation of the music form. J. Flores argues that Puerto Rican youths, as a result of the African foundations of their cultural backgrounds and similar effects of postindustrialization in neighborhoods of New York City, most directly shared the creative stage for the development of the hip hop culture. The consumers of rap, however, include youths of all races, classes, and nationalities. Interestingly, more white suburban youths consume rap music than poor black youths. In fact, the success of the rap album *Niggaz 4 Life* as the number one selling album in the country in 1989 is attributed to its demand by middle class white youths. M. Dyson and R. Kelley suggest that for youths residing outside of inner-cities, the ghetto represents 'a place of adventure, unbridled violence, erotic fantasy and/or an imagery alternative to suburban boredom.'

The Forms of Rap Music

Basically, two forms of rap music are recognized: (1) life-line or hard-core rap; and (2) commercial or soft rap. Commercial or 'soft rap' is devoid of any social message and addresses common issues between the classes or races. The Fresh Prince's *Parents Don't Understand*, which describes the problems and frustrations that exists between parents and teenagers, is an example of soft rap.

The lyrics of hard core rap contain explicit language and violent and sexual imagery. Hard core rap consists of two subcategories: (1) political or Black nationalist rap; and (2) gangsta rap. Political or black nationalist rap draws heavily on the philosophies and doctrines of Black nationalist organizations such as the Black Panthers and the Nation of Islam, and political and religious figures such as Malcolm X,

Martin Luther King, and Marcus Garvey. Describing the social, economic and political status of Blacks, it promotes Africentrism, Black empowerment and the preservation of Black culture. Public Enemy's (PE) *Fight the Power* is an example of this subgenre.

Gangsta rap, which is the focus of most of the criticism of rap music, developed on the West Coast in the late 1980s. While it also describes the social milieu and experiences of inner city youths, it differs from political or Black nationalist rap in that its messages and themes:

1. Glorify the gangsta lifestyle and mentality. Borrowing from the characterization of white male gangsters in the 1920s, gangsta rap projects the life of the rebellious outlaw in which violence is the norm, and killing is a necessary means of survival.
2. Advocate the use of violence against women and the police.
3. Promote sexist and misogynist attitudes toward women. Women are depicted as bitches and whores who serve as the sexual objects of men or who are nags or gold diggers.
4. Promote stereotypical perceptions of the sexual prowess of black men and the black male as the crazy or psychotic nigger.

Examples of gangsta rap include Ice-T's *Cop Killer*, NWA's *Fuck the Police* and Tupac Shakur's *Outlaw*.

Although the explicit language and violent and sexual imagery form the basis of the public debate regarding the harmfulness of hard core rap, these characteristics are not exclusive to rap music nor is it a contemporary phenomenon. The criticism and censorship of popular music date back to the early 1900s. Moreover, some of the lyrics of earlier songs such as Lloyd Price's *Stagger Lee* (1958) and Alan Lomax's (1955) *Make Me a Pallet on the Floor* rival that of most modern day gangsta rappers.

The characteristics of hard core rap are also similar to those found in heavy metal music. Both contain themes of rebellion against authority and the manipulation and abuse (largely sexual) of women. According to R. Stallworth, the two music genre differ in terms of the directness in which these messages are expressed. Heavy metalists sometimes mask their messages; the messages in rap tend to be more direct. Although heavy metal music has also been criticized, as will be noted in the next section, this criticism tends to differ from that levied against rap music.

The Causation Arguments

As noted earlier, the perceived relationship between popular music and adolescent crime and delinquency is nothing new. New music has always been seen as too sexually suggestive and as dangerous to public morals. According to A. Binder, three basic arguments have been used to encourage the censorship of heavy metal and rap music: (1) the corruption of youths; (2) the protection of youths; and (3) danger to society.

The *corruption argument* states that explicit lyrics—whether glorifying suicide, anti-authority attitudes or deviant sexual acts—have a negative effect on youth's attitudes. The emphasis is the effect of the music on young listeners rather than the effect such listeners might have on society at large. In short, the music suggests to youths that these forms of behaviors are acceptable.

The *protection argument* suggests that parents and other adults must shield America's youth from offensive song lyrics. Underlying this argument are the assumptions of adult responsibility and youths' need for security and guidance in living. How to best protect youths, however, varies from suggestions of laws against harmful music to warning labels for explicit materials.

Finally, the *danger to society argument* posits that the consumers of the music pose a danger to women, teachers and other authority figures. Unlike the previous two arguments, the focus here is on the *adolescent* and not the *effects of the music on adolescent's attitudes and behaviors.*

Is Rap a Cultural Threat?

Both Binder and T. Rose note that the danger to society argument is more likely to be applied to rap music than heavy metal music. This may be associated with the perceived demographic characteristics of both the consumers and producers of the music. Rap is perceived as being an urban black (lower-class) youth music genre; heavy metal music is perceived to be the music genre of middle- and working-class white youths. Rose, in particular, argues that the assaults on rap music are part of a long-standing sociologically based discourse that positions black influences as a cultural threat to American society. Although heavy metal music is also viewed as being harmfulness to American norms and values, heavy metal fans are depicted as victims of that influence; rap fans, on the other hand, are depicted as representatives of the cultural threat. In short, the attacks on black and white youth's cultural expressions differ in important ways. Unlike heavy metal music, the ideology surrounding the harmfulness of rap music results in the criminalization of both black youths and their music.

Ignoring the Obvious Causes of Violence

The contentious debate about the relationship between music lyrics and societal behavior is surely controversial. The assertion that violent lyrics cause violent behavior is neither convincing nor conclusive. The obvious causes of social violence—economic inequality, racism, and racial profiling— are all but ignored when the focus is on the music of (minority) youth. Often the efforts to "objectively investigate" the roots of social violence amounts to little more than racial scapegoating of black and latino youth.

Michael Eric Dyson, testimony before the Senate Commerce, Science, and Transportation Committee, September 13, 2000.

Three popular incidents that have been used to illustrate the dangerousness of rap music and its consumers include (1) the New York's Central Park wilding incident where a group of inner city youths who were reported to be involved in rap music attacked a female jogger; and (2) violent juvenile attacks on police officers in North Carolina and Texas. In the North Carolina incident, the youths were found to have NWA 'Niggers with Attitude' carved on their rifle stocks. The defense attorney in the Texas case argued that his juvenile client was influenced by the lyrics of the gangsta rap song 'Fuck the Police.' The recent violent murders of gangsta rappers Tupac Shakur and The Notorious B.I.G. (AKA Christopher Wallace) have further added fuel to the debate regarding the delinquent and criminal effects of rap music.

Is there a link between the violent and sexually explicit lyrics and imagery portrayed in rap music and adolescent crime and violence? And if so, what are the dynamics of this relationship? . . .

The Empirical Evidence

Despite the public outcry against rap music, there has been surprisingly little scholarly research that has examined its effects on adolescents. In fact, a review of the extant literature reveals only nine empirical studies investigating potential links between rap music and violence, deviance, self-concept and/or social perceptions. These studies are fairly recent (most being conducted in 1994–5), and are exploratory in nature.

In possibly the first empirical study involving rap music, J. Epstein, D. Pratto and J. Skipper examined the relationship between musical preference, commitment to popular music and behavioral problems. The researchers hypothesized that: (1) musical preference was related to race; (2) musical preference predicted behavioral problems; and (3) the frequency of behavioral problems was related to the number of hours spent listening to popular music. Data collected from a survey, school records and participant observation of 80 middle school teens revealed that although race did predict musical preference—white students preferred heavy metal music, black students preferred rap music—there were no significant relationships between music type and behavioral problems or commitment to music and the frequency of behavioral problems.

K. Took and D. Weiss surveyed both adolescents and their parents to assess the association between current and past psychosocial functioning and music preferences. Adolescents in this study were outpatients at a military adolescent or private psychiatric, substance abuse counseling or residential care unit. Study findings indicated that adolescents who preferred heavy metal and rap music had higher incidence of below-average school grades, school behavior problems, sexual activity, drug and alcohol use and arrests. However, when gender was controlled, only below-averaged school grades and a history of counseling in elementary school for school problems remained significant. The researchers concluded that the correlation between music preferences and behavioral problems was a result of adolescent male socialization. Moreover, since the behavioral problems started before youths began to listen to heavy metal and rap, the researchers argued that music genres contributed to rather than caused the problems.

Studying the Impact of Music Videos

Some academic scholars suggest that music videos, which interpret or embellish a song, have a greater impact on the attitudes and activities of the consumer than audio music. Although no one has compared the differential effects of the two music treatments for rap music, researchers have assessed the effects of exposure to rap music videos on adolescent attitudes toward the use of violence. J. Johnson, L. Jackson and L. Gatto found that African American male youths (ages 11–16) who were exposed to violent rap music videos expressed a greater acceptance of the use of violence (including violence against women) than those youths who viewed nonviolent rap videos or no music videos. In another study, James Johnson and Mike Adams, Leslie Ashburn and William Reed compared the effects of exposure to nonviolent rap videos on the attitudes of teenage African American males and females toward dating violence. Sixty adolescents divided into two control and two experimental groups (15 males and 15 females per group type) viewed videos depicting women in sexually subordinate roles or saw no videos. Adolescents then read a vignette involving teen dating violence perpetuated by a male. Results showed that while male acceptance of violence was not a function of viewing the videos, video-viewing females showed greater acceptance of teen dating violence than females who viewed no videos.

D. Zillman, C. Aust, K. Hoffman, and C. Love moved beyond examining the relationship between rap music and violence to study the effects of popular rock, nonpolitical rap or radical political rap music videos on the self-esteem and voting behavior of African American and white high school students. Students' exposure to the three types of music videos and their subsequent participation in a mock student election indicated that: (1) music preferences were race specific—African American students preferred rap whereas white students preferred popular rock; (2) neither music genre affected the self-esteem or voting behavior of African American students; and (3) white students showed higher scholastic abilities after viewing rap videos and were more likely to support a liberal African American candidate after exposure to radical political rap music videos.

Studying College Students

In addition to adolescent populations, researchers have also analyzed the effects of rap music on college students and mental health patients. Interviewing a female sample enrolled at a historically black college, B. Wade and C. Thomas-Gunnar found that although the content of rap music was perceived to be inappropriate and harmful to society, it was also viewed as being reflective of the existing black gender relations. C. Barongan, G. Hall and C. Nagayama, however, found that college males who listened to misogynous rap music were more likely to show assaultive or sexually violent film vignettes to female confederates (30%) than college males who had listened to neutral rap music (7%). The link between music and antisocial and delinquent behavior was not supported in a later experiment by M. Ballard and S. Coates. Exposure to one of six songs (3 heavy metal and 3 rap) representing nonviolent, homicidal and suicidal themes did not significantly affect the suicidal ideation, anxiety or self-esteem of male or female undergraduates. In regards to the rap music, students who heard the nonviolent song reported more depressive symptoms than students who heard the violent song. Rap songs also elicited greater angry responses than heavy metal songs. The researchers attributed these findings to two factors: (1) that students felt better about their lives after hearing the violent lyrics; and (2) few students in the samples (which was primarily non-Hispanic Caucasians) reported rap as their musical preference. As for research involving mental health patients, C. Harris, R. Bradley and S. Titus reported more inappropriate behavior among patients when hard rock and rap music were played than when country and western or easy listening music were played.

To summarize, extant research, although addressing many of the issues surrounding rap music, does not consistently show that it influences attitudes and behaviors. In fact, there is almost an even split between studies that suggest that rap music has antisocial and delinquent effects and studies that suggest that these effects are minor or nonexistent. What is evident is that scholarly analysis of the topic is in its initial stages. This combined with the inherent limitations of existing studies indicate the need for further research. . . .

As revealed by the literature review, we cannot conclude with any degree of certainty that violent and sexually explicit rap lyrics lead impressionable youths to antisocial, criminal and delinquent behavior. Unfortunately, it appears that present arguments regarding the harmfulness of rap music are based on factors other than scholarly analysis. The truth of the matter is that the effects of rap music, regardless of subtype, are basically unknown. This does not mean, however, that rap music has no negative effects, direct or indirect, on youths. It does mean that extensive research must be conducted before causal inferences are made.

Periodical Bibliography

The following articles have been selected to supplement the diverse views presented in this chapter.

American Academy of Pediatrics — "Media Violence," *Pediatrics*, November 2001.

L. Brent Bozell III — "TV's Fatal Attraction," *Crisis*, February 2000.

Allan C. Brownfeld — "Television Responsible for Coarsening American Society," *Washington Inquirer*, June 15, 1998.

Guy Cumberbatch — "Only a Game?" *New Scientist*, June 10, 2000.

Jim D'Entremont — "Preachers of Doom," *Index on Censorship*, July/August 1999.

Brian Doherty — "Bum Rap: Lynne Cheney vs. Slim Shady," *Reason*, December 2000.

Christopher J. Ferguson — "Media Violence: Miscast Causality," *American Psychologist*, June/July 2002.

Jib Fowles — "The Whipping Boy," *Reason*, March 2001.

Bruce Grierson — "The Profits of Violence: There's Gold in Them There Kills," *Progressive Populist*, June 1999.

Dave Grossman — "Teaching Kids to Kill," *National Forum*, Fall 2000.

Adam Groves — "Columbine High vs. Violence 'n the Media," *Gauntlet*, 2000.

Gayle M.B. Hanson — "The Violent World of Video Games," *Insight*, June 28, 1999.

Robert Hilburn — "No Easy Answer for Violence in Gangsta Rap," *Los Angeles Times*, March 10, 1997.

Frank Keating — "Mayhem Culture," *Wall Street Journal*, April 10, 1998.

Daphne Lavers — "Media Violence: Ugly and Getting Uglier," *World & I*, March 2002.

John Leo — "When Life Imitates Video," *U.S. News & World Report*, May 3, 1999.

Robert Stacy McCain — "Television's Bloody Hands," *Insight*, December 21, 1998.

Richard Rhodes — "Hollow Claims About Fantasy Violence," *New York Times*, September 17, 2000.

Stephanie Stapleton — "Media Violence Is Harmful to Kids—and to Public Health," *American Medical News*, August 24, 2000.

Shelby Steele — "Notes from the Hip-Hop Underground," *Wall Street Journal*, March 30, 2001.

Jacob Sullum — "All *Doom* Players Aren't Homicidal Maniacs," *Conservative Chronicle*, June 2, 1999.

CHAPTER 2

Should the
Government Restrict
Media Violence?

Chapter Preface

All media forms have met with public scrutiny, but since its inception, television has met with particular scorn. After World War II, television had penetrated most American homes, and by 1960, children were spending more time with television than with radios, comic books, or playmates. People became concerned about the influence that television—especially violent programs—might have on children, and social scientists began to study television's effects. Because regulation of television is thought by many to be a violation of free speech, the government has been reluctant to do more than chastise television broadcasters for violent programming. Television's impact continues to ignite public concern, however, and to stir legislative efforts to restrict television violence.

Despite the meager evidence available during the 1950s, social scientists of that era claimed that there was reason to to be concerned about television's influence. In 1961, however, Wilbur Schram, Jack Lyle, and Edwin Parker published the results of their study, *Television in the Lives of Our Children*. The study concluded that "for most children, under most conditions, most television is probably neither harmful nor particularly beneficial." Nevertheless, commentators continued to cite television as a factor contributing to societal violence. In response to these concerns, the government began to rebuke industry leaders. In 1961, the Federal Communications Commission (FCC) chairman Newton Minow told the National Association of Broadcasters that they had made television into a "vast wasteland" of overly violent programming. The U.S. government was still reluctant to pass laws restricting television's content, however. Instead, Minow asked that broadcasters voluntarily improve television programming, especially for children.

During the 1970s and 1980s, scientists conducted thousands of studies on the effects of television violence. The office of the surgeon general and the National Institute of Mental Health compiled the results in reports that claimed a link between television violence and aggression. Despite these claims, the administration of President Ronald Reagan continued to oppose any regulation. In 1983 FCC chairman

Mark Fowler told the *Washington Post* that television should not be regulated any more than other home appliances, calling the television a "toaster with pictures."

Public concern over television violence remained, however, and studies purporting to establish the link between violent programming and aggression continued to be published. Former FCC chairman Minow expressed his growing concern: "In 1961, I worried that my children would not benefit much from television, but in 1991 I worry that my grandchildren will actually be harmed by it." Nevertheless, constitutional authorities continued to argue that any restriction on the television industry risked censorship, and political leaders and community activists could only plead with television broadcasters to come up with a plan to deal with the problem of television violence.

Finally, in the 1990s, the federal government did pass a law aimed at helping parents protect their children from violent programming, although the law was not a restriction on violent content itself. After years of hearings and debate, in 1996 President Bill Clinton signed the Telecommunications Act into law. The act required broadcasters to develop a rating system for their programs and television manufacturers to include V-chips—a computer chip that allows parents to control violent programming on their own television—in all television sets. The industry developed a ratings system in 1997 that the FCC approved in 1998; the V-chip became available in 1999.

Public anxiety about television violence continues to generate calls for regulation. Some analysts now equate the violence on television with pollution and seek action similar to that leveled at the tobacco industry, which has been sued by those harmed by its products. These commentators claim that the First Amendment, which protects speech, does not protect industries that produce pollution that harms America's children. Whether this harm is sufficient to censor television programs, however, remains the subject of intense debate.

Whether or not the government should restrict the violence on television or in any media continues to be hotly debated. The authors of the viewpoints in the following chapter express their opinions on this controversial issue.

*"If successful, [lawsuits against the media]
would substantively reduce the scope of
First Amendment protection."*

Government Restriction of Media Violence Threatens Free Speech

Paul McMasters

Government efforts to restrict violent content in entertainment threaten to undermine the First Amendment, argues Paul McMasters in the following viewpoint. Labeling violent content as dangerous speech and holding the entertainment industry financially accountable for any violence resulting from their products, he claims, will reduce the scope of protected speech. According to McMasters, Americans risk sacrificing their right to speak their own minds when they allow the government to restrict speech they find offensive. McMasters is First Amendment Ombudsman for the Freedom Forum First Amendment Center at Vanderbilt University.

As you read, consider the following questions:

1. According to McMasters, what is the freedom Americans value most?
2. In the author's opinion, what hurdles must be overcome to demonstrate that media violence can provoke actual violence?
3. What does McMasters claim is the visceral response to provocative speech?

The United States Senate Rules Committee has been debating whether to create a special committee, task force or commission on American culture. The sponsors of the proposal want to inquire into whether Hollywood entertainment is creating a violent and profane culture that threatens the morality of America's youth.

Curbing Entertainment

This is the most recent in a series of congressional initiatives to curb perceived excesses in the entertainment media and a general coarsening of public life. Some of those other initiatives:

- The Federal Trade Commission has issued subpoenas to movie and record producers in an investigation into whether they are violating their own voluntary ratings system in marketing to young people.
- The U.S. Surgeon General has been directed by President Bill Clinton to inquire into the effects of popular entertainment on young people.
- Congress is considering the creation of a national commission on youth violence that would look into popular culture's impact on the behavior of teen-agers; other proposals would create a standard rating system for all media.

There are similar stirrings across the nation.

State legislatures have taken up literally hundreds of bills that would regulate the Internet, movie theaters, video stores, computer games, records and CDs, concerts, books, magazines and comics, what children wear to school. The targets are sex, violence, hate speech, music lyrics, mayhem, incivility and a variety of other expressive activities that employ words, images, and ideas.

This activity in the state and federal legislatures reflects the deep concerns of millions of citizens who believe our culture is too cluttered with negative influences. Just a few examples:

- A group that calls itself Morality in Media launched a national campaign this summer against racy magazines such as *Cosmopolitan*, *Redbook*, *Marie Claire* and *Glamour* near checkout counters in stores.
- A number of groups are pushing for the posting of the

Ten Commandments in schools and other public places.

- In hundreds of communities, there are battles over prayer in schools and at graduation and athletic events as well as over whether creationism should be taught in public schools.
- Other groups and individuals are worried about the messages their children are getting from toys, such as Teletubbies, Barbie dolls and the Pokemon paraphernalia.

There is a long list of such examples, which seem to prove a rather widespread preoccupation with public order and personal morality driven by a popular estrangement from First Amendment traditions.

Usually the target in these citizen campaigns is speech that is considered offensive and threatening. Falsely shouting fire in a crowded theater was the compelling illustration Justice Oliver Wendell Holmes used in *Schenck v. United States* (1920) as a classic example of speech that was unprotected because it could provoke dangerous and injurious action.

Too Much Freedom?

So, what is causing all the current turmoil over expressive activities that some consider dangerously provocative?

Is it because there is more offensive and threatening speech today than there used to be? Or are we more easily offended or frightened than we used to be? Or is it a little of both?

What is the significance of this activity? Are we just in a temporary panic that will eventually subside? Or are we contemplating profound changes in the way we live as individuals and as a society?

When Americans are asked in national surveys which freedom they most value, the overwhelming majority says freedom of speech. Which raises the question of why have these proposals to limit freedom of speech gained so much currency?

Have Americans come to the conclusion that they have too much freedom? Whatever the answers, the questions go right to our constitutional core, which is the Bill of Rights in general and the First Amendment in particular, since it is arguably the amendment that secures the life of the other nine.

The Bill of Rights is the 10 amendments imposed as a

condition on the ratification of the Constitution. The states and anti-federalists wanted to guarantee fundamental freedoms for individual citizens to protect them from the power of government, the will of the majority, or the passion of the moment.

So, the Constitution lays out what the government can do and the Bill of Rights lays out what the government cannot do.

In other words, the Constitution defines us as a nation. The Bill of Rights defines us as a people. . . .

Threats Against the First Amendment

A number of cases now working their way through the judicial system could result in a[n] evisceration of the First Amendment's protection for extreme or incendiary speech. These cases include:

- *Byers v. Edmondson et al.:* In this case, the family of a young woman shot by a young couple claims that the Oliver Stone movie *Natural Born Killers* influenced the killers. The Louisiana Supreme Court rejected a motion for dismissal and the case is expected to go to trial sometime in 2000. [On June 6, 2002, the Louisiana Court of Appeals held that the film was protected speech.]

- *Amedure v. Telepictures Productions et al.:* In May 1999, a Michigan jury awarded the family of Scott Amedure $25 million. The young man was killed after the taping of a Jenny Jones Show episode during which he revealed he had a crush on Jonathan Schmitz, later convicted of the slaying. The family claimed in the suit against the show that the producers were negligent.

- *Planned Parenthood v. American Coalition of Life Activists:* In early 1999, a Portland, Oregon, jury ruled that an Internet Web site known as The Nuremberg Files was liable for $110,000 in damages because the virulently anti-abortion speech on the site constituted a threat to abortion providers. [On May 16, 2002, the 9th Circuit U.S. Court of Appeals upheld the lower court's verdict.]

- *James et al. v. Meow Media Inc. et al.:* On April 12, 1999, parents of three students killed at Heath High School in Paducah, Kentucky, filed a $130 million lawsuit against

Internet sites, computer-game companies and the makers and distributors of the 1995 movie *The Basketball Diaries*. They claim that these media influenced freshman Michael Carneal, who was convicted of killing the three students and wounding five others. [On August 13, 2002, the 6th Circuit U.S. Court of Appeals upheld the dismissal of the suit against the media defendants.]

These cases demonstrate that no medium is immune from such suits. They target movies, television, the Internet, and video games. More importantly, if successful, they would substantively reduce the scope of First Amendment protection by expanding the definitions of such legal concepts as incitement, threat, intent, negligence, reasonable person and foresight.

The Right to Do Wrong

Today's media, at their worst, are certainly as appalling as their severest critics say. But that is neither here nor there. If freedom is to survive, the media must have the right to do wrong.

Nor can this be only a nominal right. When government was smaller, one could simply defend the right of revolting people not to be subjected to obvious and overt coercion. Today, we are called to a much harder task. Because government now invades people's lives by any plausible means, on any plausible excuse, we must work with those we actively despise to ensure they are not denied by indirect methods any reasonable means of exercising their rights to the full.

Roger Donway, *Navigator*, February 2001.

At the heart of lawsuits challenging incendiary speech is the idea that violence in the media causes violence in people or on the street. That has not been proved, of course, because studies that indicate a link between viewing violence and doing violence turn out to be quite qualified in both their methodology and their conclusions.

There are significant hurdles to demonstrating that media violence can provoke actual violence, among them: Children form basic values at a very young age based primarily on family influence and early environment. There is no way to safely predict whether a given stimulus, violent or nonviolent, will provoke positive, negative or no conduct, given the vagaries of human personalities.

Is Media Violence a Threat?

But even if studies were to demonstrate a causal link between violence in the media and violence in a small portion of the populace, the question arises: Would that be sufficient incentive to reduce all expression to that which wouldn't influence a six-year-old or incite a sociopath?

Finally, these cases share . . . the idea that some speech is just too hot to handle. That it is like shouting fire in a crowded theater. That it is too dangerous and provocative.

The visceral response to such speech, of course, is to prevent it, or failing that, to punish it until it stops. We would do that in the name of good social order, cleaning up the culture, silencing speech that offends or threatens some citizens.

What have the courts said so far? Generally, that fighting words, incitement and threats are not always protected by the First Amendment. But the exceptions for the most part have been carefully defined and narrowly construed. For example, there have been a number of suits against motion pictures for copycat crimes in the last 15 years; none has been upheld by the courts.

Even so, when movie producers and others are forced to expend large sums to defend themselves, protected speech is both punished and chilled.

Where does the campaign against incendiary speech take us? . . .

If the court cases reviewed here are successful, they could generate a blizzard of litigation. Under those circumstances, is any creative work safe?

Remember, Timothy McVeigh was supposed to have used the racist novel *The Turner Diaries* as a blueprint for the Oklahoma City bombing. Theodore Kaczynski, the so-called Unabomber, was supposed to have been inspired by Joseph Conrad novels. Mark Chapman, the man who killed John Lennon, was supposed to have been motivated by J.D. Salinger's writings. Comic books and rock 'n' roll reportedly drove the murderous rampage of Charles Starkweather [who with his girlfriend Caril Ann Fugate conducted a killing spree from Nebraska to Wyoming in 1958].

If these cases survive, they take root in constitutional jurisprudence and lie in wait for yet another act of expression that someone mistakes for an incitement to violence.

The idea that we can blame books, movies and other media for crime turns the courtroom search for justice into a search for blame and deep pockets. In such an environment, what people read or watch or listen to becomes not an act of enlightenment or entertainment but a call to commit violence. What is in the mind of the creator of such works becomes synonymous with what is in the heart of the killer.

All of this presents an enormous challenge: Can the First Amendment, which has served us so well for more than 200 years, survive in its present form? It is not beyond possibility that deterioration of our First Amendment sensibility and hypersensitivity to the speech of others will create an anti-speech virus that worms its way to our constitutional heart. Can we rise to such challenges or do we let them lead us into a new millennium where we'll be less free but more comfortable?

There are a series of ironies in these conundrums:
- That a First Amendment that has served us so well for two centuries will come to be considered something that Americans can get along without.
- That in so vigorously asserting their "right" not to be offended or frightened, Americans will undermine their right to speak their minds and hold strong opinions.
- That in equating extreme speech as something harmful like guns, tobacco and pollution, Americans will forget that unlike the human body the human mind can be improved by negative influence.

When it comes to speech, even the odious can inform and energize and provoke a positive response. But a significant number of Americans seem to have reached a point where they are quite ready to trade their freedom for a little more civility and security.

Down that road lies cultural homogeneity, social and intellectual stagnation, and the possibility that we will be not only living with the tyranny of the majority but the tyranny of the aggrieved, also.

"Most politicians and parents don't favor censorship . . . but there is greater and greater support for promoting parental empowerment."

Government Restriction of Media Violence Does Not Threaten Free Speech

Joanne Cantor

In the following viewpoint Joanne Cantor argues that government actions restricting violent media are not censorship but provide parents with the necessary information to protect their children. Research shows that media violence is harmful to children, Cantor maintains, but simply communicating the dangers of media violence is often not enough. Requiring that violent programs be labeled and that televisions be equipped with a V-chip that identifies violent programs does not censor the media, she claims, but helps parents monitor what their children watch. Cantor is professor of communication arts at the University of Wisconsin, in Madison.

As you read, consider the following questions:

1. In Cantor's opinion, why are fewer parents aware of the television ratings system in 2000 than they were in 1997?
2. According to the author, what is the greatest obstacle to communicating the message that media violence involves mental health risks?
3. What two functions are served by writing letters of complaint to local newspapers, in Cantor's opinion?

Violence has been a staple of media entertainment for as long as we've had "mass media." And although concerns about media violence go back as far as the 1930s with movies, the denunciations have never been as fierce as they've been since the April 20, 1999, Columbine school shootings in Littleton, Colorado. In spite of the mounting evidence of harm, the entertainment industries continue to deny their role. Even though almost every public health organization now agrees that exposure to media violence has unhealthy effects, a large portion of the public is still confused about the issue. . . .

Media Violence Contributes to Youth Violence

Although most people agree that many unhealthy influences come together when a child commits criminal violence, research has shown that media violence is one of the significant contributors to violent behavior. Of course, researchers cannot do experiments in which they randomly assign children to watch different doses of violent programming throughout their youth and then observe which of them committed violent crimes as adults. But they have other powerful ways of showing the connection between viewing violence and aggressive behavior. First, they do longitudinal surveys of what children watch and look at the types of behaviors they engage in over time. They control for other factors, such as previous aggressiveness, family background, and the like. And they find a consistent correlation between violence viewing and violent behavior, even controlling for other influences. They also do experiments, which compare the behavior of children who are randomly assigned to view an excerpt of a violent or nonviolent program or movie. These studies show short-term effects, such as increases in hostility, more accepting attitudes toward violence, or an increased willingness to inflict harm—changes that we know raise the likelihood of violent actions, both in the short term and in the long run. A meta-analysis, which statistically combined the findings of all the relevant studies, makes a compelling case that media violence consistently contributes to violent behavior.

Viewing violence promotes violence in a variety of ways.

First, research shows that children often copy what they see in the media. Some critics of this research argue that the observed effects are trivial. Indeed, some frequently-quoted "classic" studies show that children who watch people punching Bobo Dolls copy that behavior, which in the end, doesn't hurt anyone. But research has demonstrated the serious consequences of imitating television violence. For example, a national survey of Israeli middle-schools showed that when World Wrestling Federation (WWF) was introduced to Israeli TV in 1994, the widespread imitation of the wrestlers' behavior produced an epidemic of serious playground injuries (including concussions and broken bones). And the children who injured their peers were old enough to tell you that they knew that what they were watching was fake. This knowledge didn't stop them from copying the wrestlers' moves anyway. The mayhem produced by WWF continued until the program's air time was substantially reduced and educators offered media literacy education to counteract the show's impact.

In addition to imitating new behaviors, children often show changes in their attitudes toward violence as a function of the way violence is presented. When televised stories show that violence is a safe, easy method to get what you want, when it produces only minor harm and is rarely punished, and when it is performed by attractive heroes or shown in a humorous context, viewers are more likely to imitate it. Systematic analyses of the content of television reveal that a high proportion of violence on television exhibits these features. Unfortunately, programs that target young children, and particularly cartoons, contain an especially high degree of this type of aggression-promoting content.

Other effects of video violence are as important as increases in aggressive behavior. One common effect is desensitization. As a result of repeated exposure to media violence as entertainment, children often become less emotionally disturbed by it. As a consequence, they show a reduced tendency to try to stop others from becoming violent, and they show less and less sympathy for the victims of violence. There is special concern about the desensitizing effect of violent video games, and the latest research shows that these concerns are well-placed. In addition to repeated desensitization experiences, many of these games provide strong reinforcements for aggressive behavior: They award points for killing the enemy and some involve scenarios in which the only way the player can "survive" is by quickly shooting each new enemy as soon as he appears. Media violence also engenders hostility in viewers. Some people argue that the well-substantiated correlation between aggressiveness and viewing violence simply shows that children who are hostile to begin with are more likely to choose violence. The fact is that the relationship goes both ways: Violent, hostile people are more avid consumers of media violence, and viewing violence increases their hostility further. Research also shows that repeated exposure to intense media violence produces a continuing hostile mental framework, causing viewers to be more likely to interpret an entirely neutral interaction as provocation, and to behave aggressively as a result. This effect occurs not just shortly after viewing violence, but even after considerable delays.

I believe that one reason many parents don't take media violence seriously is that few of us envision our children ever committing criminal violence, and, of course, only a tiny percentage of children do. So much attention is paid to criminal violence that other important effects are ignored. Some of the other effects of viewing violence, such as desensitization and increased hostility, affect a much higher proportion of children. Parents need to be made aware of these important, unhealthy potential outcomes of viewing so that they will understand that heavy exposure to media violence has harmful effects on most children.

Media Violence Is Scary

Another important effect of media violence is fear. This is an effect I've been studying for almost two decades, and other researchers have focused on this issue as well. A 1998 survey of elementary and middle school children revealed that as hours of television viewing increased, so did the symptoms of anxiety, depression, and posttraumatic stress. Similarly, a 1999 survey of the parents of elementary school children revealed that the amount of children's television viewing (especially television viewing at bedtime) and having a television in their own bedroom, were significantly related to the frequency of children's sleep disturbances. Indeed, almost 10% of the parents surveyed reported that their child experienced TV-induced nightmares *at least once a week*. . . .

Limiting Exposure

Given the established harms that can come from viewing violence, it's surprising that there's so much of it in our entertainment culture. The disturbing truth is, however, that media violence is an enormously profitable business, and all signs point to the media becoming even more violent in the future. Because media violence is so pervasive, and even the children of highly vigilant and involved parents are likely to be exposed to media violence sometimes, it is important to understand how to protect children from its effects. Parents need guidance in finding ways to limit their children's exposure and to counteract the effects of what their children do see. In addition, parents, teachers, administrators, and community members need to join together and speak out for greater parental empowerment in this area.

Fortunately, ratings and labels to inform parents about the media content their children might see are becoming increasingly available. Motion picture ratings (which now include G, PG, PG-13, R, and NC-17) have been used since the 1960s to suggest the appropriate age for viewing theatrical films. These ratings have been criticized for being vague and for not giving information about the content of movies, information that parents overwhelmingly prefer to age recommendations. As a result of public pressure, starting in 1995, the Motion Picture Association of America has been providing information about the content that was responsible for a movie's rating on its web site (www.mpaa.org).

Regulating Ratings

Ratings for television programs, a new tool for parents, were instituted beginning in 1997. Producers rate their own programs, and although the ratings are technically voluntary, they are intended to be applied to all programming with the exception of news and sports. The rating system, called the

TV Parental Guidelines, was designed by the television industry and modeled after the movie ratings. The original system had six levels based on the appropriateness of a program for different age groups. These levels are TV-Y (All Children), TV-Y7 (Directed to Older Children), TV-G (General Audience), TV-PG (Parental Guidance Suggested), TV-14 (Parents Strongly Cautioned), and TV-MA (Mature Audience Only). After receiving intense criticism in the six months after it was implemented, the rating system was amended to add content information to the age-based ratings. The revision added FV for "fantasy violence" in children's programs, and V, S, L, and D, for violence, sex, coarse language, and sexual dialogue, respectively, in general audience programs. The ratings are displayed visually in the upper left-hand corner of the television screen for the first few seconds of a program. They are also available in some newspaper television listings. The amended system is now quite complicated, and the television industry has done very little to publicize it. In fact, research shows that in the year 2000, fewer parents are aware of the television rating system than knew about it in 1997.

Parents Are Concerned About Violent Content on TV

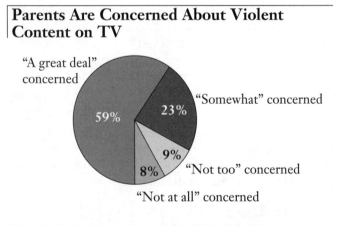

"A great deal" concerned

"Somewhat" concerned

59%

23%

9%

8%

"Not too" concerned

"Not at all" concerned

Kaiser Family Foundation, *Parents and the V-Chip*, July 2001.

Television ratings were made necessary by the Telecommunications Act of 1996, which mandated that all new televisions with a screen size of thirteen inches or larger be manufactured with another new tool for parental empowerment, the V-chip. By January of 2000 all television manufacturers were complying with this mandate. The V-chip is a device that permits parents to block programs as a function of their ratings. In spite of the complicated nature of the TV rating system, the V-chip can be very helpful to parents. By using the V-chip, parents can keep some programs out of their homes automatically. For example, parents can let their children watch *Sesame Street* or *Blues Clues* and not worry that they will inadvertently stumble into *Jerry Springer* or *The X-Files*. If a child wants to watch a program that is blocked, he or she simply has to get permission from mom or dad, since the blocking can be overridden by entering a private PIN number. Many sets then return to the previous settings for blocking programs the next time the television is turned off. In addition, some V-chips provide further protection by allowing parents to block unrated programs as well as programs with ratings. Many television sets also allow parents to block entire channels, and some systems allow programs to be blocked by title or time of day. V-chips that can be added to an older TV set are also available. More advanced systems are now being developed that will allow parents to select or block programs according their own concerns on the basis of ratings assigned by independent coders rather than TV producers. . . .

Joining Together

One of the greatest challenges to groups concerned with media violence is that it is difficult to communicate the message that media violence involves mental health risks. The greatest obstacle is that the media industries, which control the most effective way to communicate to a large audience, have a tremendous economic stake in media violence and are averse to disseminating our message. The obstruction is worse than just making it difficult for media violence critics to receive air time; in their coverage of the issue, the media repeatedly deny the established conclusions of research. For this reason, it is all the more important for schools and other grass-roots organizations to communicate with each other and with their members and stake-holders. This is also one reason I've put university teaching behind me and have dedicated a good deal of my time to communicating with parents, schools, and mental health and childcare specialists on the issue.

School personnel need to communicate with parents. Many teachers and school social workers tell me that they can see the effects of children's viewing spilling over into the classroom and the playground, but they find it difficult to enlist the parents' cooperation in finding solutions. Even many parents who are aware of the risks have found that "just saying 'no'" can backfire. So in addition to understanding the risks, parents need to learn strategies for enlisting their children's cooperation in making healthy media choices.

Parents need to talk to one another. Guiding their own children's viewing at home is only part of the process. Enlisting the cooperation of the parents of their children's friends is necessary, too. Other parents may find concerns about TV violence odd or "old fashioned" if they are unaware of the well-documented risks.

Children and adolescents need to be involved in the dialogue, too, in classrooms, in after-school activities, and in homes. Discussions can range from components of formal media literacy curricula to spontaneous responses to incidents in the school or to events in the media. Helping children to question the values that the media promote, as well as to become critical of their own choices for entertainment can encourage them to become more discerning adult media consumers.

Speaking Out

Beyond speaking to each other, we need to speak out to the media industries in ways they will understand and heed. I often hear television station managers saying that they rarely get complaints about violence. Some say that when they've aired something controversial but have heard no protests, they took it as an endorsement and went on to present more of the same. It's important to pick up the phone and call a local station that airs something inappropriate or unhealthy in a context where many children are watching. An even better option is writing a letter to the station with copies to the local paper. If the paper prints it, the complaint will serve two functions—giving the station the negative feedback it needs and alerting other parents to problems they might not be aware of. And as more and more TV's have blocking capabilities, joining together to block a channel that is unresponsive to legitimate complaints may become a parent-action tactic of the future.

Empowerment, Not Censorship

National politicians are responsive to parental input as well. Having testified before both houses of Congress, I know that TV ratings and the V-chip were made possible only because members of congress were hearing the concerns of their constituents. Most politicians and parents don't favor censorship (I certainly don't), but there is greater and greater support for promoting parental empowerment. The Federal Trade Commission is investigating the marketing of violence to children, and a bill [the 21st Century Media Responsibility Act of 1999, reintroduced in May 2001] was introduced in Congress that would regulate the labeling of violent content in video games and other new media.

It is important to remember that actions like these do not amount to censorship—they do not prevent content from being produced or distributed; they simply help parents have a say in what their own children are exposed to. This is not censorship—it's a move toward returning parenting power to parents.

Most importantly, the greatest means we have to protect our children is through the promotion of public education. If public attitudes toward children's unfettered access to media violence can move in the direction of attitudes toward smoking or driving without a seatbelt, we will have made huge strides toward raising a healthier generation of young people.

"The [Media Marketing Accountability Act] does not in any way allow the FTC to regulate the content of movies, music, or video games."

The Government Should Restrict Media Marketed to Children

Joe Lieberman

In the following viewpoint Joe Lieberman, a U.S. Senator from Connecticut and sponsor of the Media Marketing Accountability Act of 2001, argues that the act does not regulate the content of entertainment but merely establishes penalties for those companies who target children when marketing violent, adult-rated entertainment. Lieberman contends that the Act is necessary because some entertainment industries market adult-rated movies, music, and video games to children. According to Lieberman, the act authorizes the Federal Trade Commission to impose penalties only when companies market products to children that the companies themselves have rated inappropriate for children according to a voluntary ratings system. As of January 2003, the act was still being considered by the Senate.

As you read, consider the following questions:
1. According to Joe Lieberman, what is the Media Marketing Accountability Act designed to do?
2. In the author's opinion, how does the act define "targeted advertising"?
3. What does Lieberman claim is the purpose of the "safe harbor" provision?

Joe Lieberman, *The Media Marketing Accountability Act: A Basic Summary*, Press Office of United States Senator Joe Lieberman, April 26, 2001.

What Is the Purpose of the Bill? To stop entertainment companies from deceptively marketing adult-rated products to children, and thus help parents better protect their kids from potentially harmful materials.[1]

Understanding the Purpose of the Bill

Why Is the Bill Needed? Last year the Federal Trade Commission (FTC) found that the movie, music, and video game industries were undermining their voluntary rating systems and deceiving parents by routinely and aggressively marketing heavily violent, adult-rated products to children. To fix this problem, the FTC called on these industries to adopt voluntary, uniform policies expressly prohibiting this practice and to enforce these policies with real sanctions for violations. Unfortunately, as the FTC noted in a follow-up report released on April 24 [2001], only the video game industry has agreed to adopt such a marketing code. The FTC also noted that, despite some encouraging changes in behavior since the release of the FTC's original report [in the fall of 2000], a number of companies in all three industries have continued to market adult-rated products in venues popular with children.

What Would the Bill Do? The FTC has the authority under current law to bring actions against businesses that engage in false and deceptive advertising practices. But the FTC's lawyers have concluded that the Commission's authority does not extend to this specific deceptive practice. The Media Marketing Accountability Act is designed to fill that gap in the law, and would apply the same rules and penalties under current law to entertainment companies that target the marketing of adult-rated products directly to children.

How Would the Bill Work? It would define the "targeted advertising or other marketing" of adult-rated movies, music recordings, and video games to minors as a deceptive act or practice under the Federal Trade Commission Act, making it illegal. It would then authorize the FTC to enforce

---

1. The bill was still being considered by the Senate when this volume went to press in August 2003.

this ban by levying civil fines against companies that label products as appropriate or suitable only for adults and then market those products to children.

Defining the Terms

What Is "Targeted Advertising"? The bill would prohibit entertainment companies from engaging in advertising or marketing that is: A) intentionally directed at minors; B) presented in venues where children comprise a "substantial proportion" of the audience; or C) otherwise directed or targeted to minors as determined by the FTC. The FTC would be authorized to develop criteria for making these determinations.

What Is "Adult-Rated"? The bill would apply to movies, music recordings and video games that carry voluntary ratings or labels indicating that: A) the product is appropriate or suitable only for adults; B) access to the product by minors should be restricted; or C) in the case of music recordings, which do not carry age-based ratings, the product may contain "explicit content." Under the existing industry rating and labeling systems, this definition would cover R-rated movies, M-rated video games, and music recordings that have a parental advisory label.

What Is a "Minor"? The bill outlaws the marketing of adult-rated material to minors, and defines a minor as "an individual below the age established under the rating or labeling system in question to be an appropriate audience for adult-oriented material, but in no event includes an individual 17 years of age or older."

Examining the Outcomes

What Will the Penalties Be? The FTC would be authorized to penalize entertainment companies that market adult-rated materials to children in the same manner and with the same means as any other company that engages in a deceptive act or practice. The Commission could choose to issue a cease and desist order. Or it could levy civil penalties of up to $11,000 per day for each specific violation, depending on the nature of the violation.

Who Decides What Is Appropriate for Children? The bill does not in any way allow the FTC to regulate the content of movies, music, or video games, nor does it allow the FTC to make judgments about the appropriateness of individual products for children. Instead, it simply authorizes the FTC to intervene in cases where companies make a representation through a voluntary rating that a product is inappropriate or unsuitable for children and then turn around and market that product directly to children.

Varvel. © 1999 by Gary Varvel. Reprinted with permission.

Will the Bill Discourage Self-Regulation? The goal of the bill is to set and enforce standards where these industries have failed to do so. It is not our intent to penalize or punish industries, such as the video game manufacturers, that have made a commitment to abide by and enforce a uniform policy prohibiting the marketing of adult-rated material to children. To make that point clear, the bill includes a "safe harbor" provision that exempts companies from FTC enforcement if they are adhering to a self-regulatory system that: A) rates products based on age appropriateness; B) prohibits the marketing of adult-rated products to children; and C) sanctions companies that do not comply with the system.

How Soon Will the Bill Take Effect? The ban on the marketing of adult-rated material to children goes into effect 90 days after enactment. The bill then gives the FTC one year from the date of enactment to develop rules for implementing the bill's requirements.

How Do We Know If the Bill Is Working? In addition to authorizing the FTC to bring actions against companies that deceptively market adult-rated material to children, the bill directs the FTC to study how well the movie, music, and video game industries are complying with the law. Specifically, it calls on the FTC to issue a report no later than two years after enactment to determine to what extent these industries are targeting adult-rated materials to children, and also to what extent movie theaters and retailers have policies and procedures to enforce the age-based ratings at the point of purchase.

"Backed by the crippling financial penalties for 'unfair or deceptive acts or practices,' [the FTC] would be able to decide which music and movies . . . would be released."

The Government Should Not Restrict Media Marketed to Children

Danny Goldberg

The Media Marketing Accountability Act of 2001 gives the Federal Trade Commission (FTC) the power to determine media content, argues Danny Goldberg in the following viewpoint. Giving the FTC the power to determine what entertainment can be mass-marketed to children determines the economic viability of content and, therefore, restricts the content that the entertainment industry will produce, Goldberg maintains. The act was still being considered by the Senate when this volume went to press. Goldberg is chairman/CEO of the independent record company Artemis Records.

As you read, consider the following questions:

1. What examples does Goldberg provide to support the argument that the entertainment industry may not be evading the ratings system?
2. In the author's opinion, what is the difference between Eminem's character Slim Shady and David Chase's character Tony Soprano?
3. According to Goldberg, what is the risk of supporting entertainment-bashing legislation?

Danny Goldberg, "The Joe and Hil Follies," *The Nation*, September 17, 2001. Copyright © 2001 by The Nation Magazine/The Nation Company, Inc. Reproduced by permission.

Two of the most famous figures in the Democratic Party, Senators Joseph Lieberman and Hillary Clinton, have introduced the Media Marketing Accountability Act of 2001, which, among other things, would make it illegal to market or promote adult-rated rap and rock-and-roll albums to kids under 17 and would empower the Federal Trade Commission (FTC) to decide which R-rated films may be marketed to minors.[1]

In April 2001, Senator Clinton said, "If you label something as inappropriate for children and then go out and target it to children, you are engaging in false and deceptive advertising." And in the summer of 2001 Democrats, occasionally joined by some Republicans, have browbeaten entertainment-industry leaders at Congressional hearings, accusing them of evading the rating system and selling salacious material to young people. But the R rating on films doesn't mean kids under 17 shouldn't see them; it means they shouldn't see them without an adult. Many parents want their kids to see such R-rated films as *Billy Elliot* and *Erin Brockovich*. As for records, the "parental advisory" sticker informs the buyer that the record contains profanity, but it does not have an age recommendation.

Regulating Content

Lieberman disingenuously says, "We're not asking the FTC to regulate content in any way, or even to make judgments about what products are appropriate for children." But that's precisely what his radical bill does. It empowers the FTC to "establish the criteria" for new ratings for records and films, and would legally require record companies and film studios to create and implement "an age-based rating or labeling system." Marketing would be deemed to be targeting minors if "the Commission determines that the advertising or marketing is otherwise directed or targeted to minors." With the FTC defining marketing to minors on the basis of FTC-mandated ratings criteria, backed by the crippling financial penalties for "unfair or deceptive acts or practices," it would

---

1. The act was still being considered by the Senate in August 2003 when this volume went to press.

be able to decide which music and movies could be mass-marketed and thus, by and large, which ones would be released. Lieberman and Clinton apparently believe that federal bureaucrats are the ideal arbiters of the appropriateness of entertainment for teenagers. Lieberman told Inside.com, "We know the difference between *Schindler's List* and *Saving Private Ryan* and some of the slasher flicks that are aimed at teenage boys. That's a decision best left to the administrative agency."

Marketing Violent Entertainment Should Not Be a Crime

Once you define violent or sexually explicit media as toxic products, it is not terribly difficult to justify regulating their advertising, at least, if not their distribution and production. Commercial speech generally enjoys constitutional protection, but as advocates of marketing restrictions assert, the First Amendment does not protect false or misleading advertising or ads promoting illegal activities. That's true but not necessarily relevant. . . . Campaigns marketing violent entertainment to children may be sleazy, but they don't promote an illegal activity (the sale of violent material to minors is not generally criminal); and they're not deceptive or unfair (many popular entertainments are just as bad as they purport to be). Ratings are not determined or mandated by the government (not yet, anyway), so why should it be a federal offense for industry executives to violate the spirit of their own voluntary codes?

Wendy Kaminer, *American Prospect*, October 23, 2000.

Two days before the legislation was introduced, the FTC issued a surreal report that criticized record companies for advertising stickered albums on the World Wrestling Federation TV show *SmackDown!* because 36 percent of its audience is under 18. So according to the FTC it's OK for younger teens to watch guys knocking the living daylights out of each other, but it's not OK to sell rap music to those same kids! Not surprisingly, more than 70 percent of the albums the FTC monitored were by African-American artists. (The FTC also included the rock band Rage Against the Machine, whose lyrics are frequently political, on the list.) At the Hip-Hop

Summit in June [2001], attended by African-American leaders including Cornel West, Martin Luther King III, Louis Farrakhan and several black members of Congress, even those who criticized the content of certain albums agreed that this legislation is dangerous and unfair.

While the FTC investigation was conducted in response to the Columbine [High School] murders [in Littleton, Colorado, on April 20, 1999], Lieberman is a one-man slippery slope who makes no bones about his desire to regulate nonviolent dirty words, complaining that "the leading music companies . . . have been doing little if anything to respond to the FTC report and curb the marketing of obscenity-laced records to kids."

Attacking Youth Culture

Although the Washington elite focuses its rhetoric on corporations, young people view these outbursts as attacks on youth culture. Just as baby boomers didn't view Bob Dylan and the Beatles as "products" of CBS and EMI, today's young people view rap and rock music as their own culture, which appears to be precisely what middle-aged pundits hate about it. George Will, for example, castigated rap lyrics [in September 2000] on ABC's *This Week*. Six months later, Will lavished praise on Sopranos executive producer David Chase for his creation. Both Eminem's Slim Shady and Chase's Tony Soprano are violent, bigoted characters whose humanity and contradictions are nonetheless illuminated by their creators. The primary difference is that rap is the cultural language of young people.

Obviously, people of good will disagree about culture, and there is nothing wrong with fierce criticism of any genre. But Lieberman et al. want to go far beyond criticism. They want government to have veto power over the marketing, and thus the economic viability, of entertainment.

By supporting this legislation Democrats may pick up a few "swing voters" who like the symbolism of entertainment-bashing, but in doing so they risk alienating young voters, fans of pop culture of all ages and civil libertarians. It is hard to imagine the young people who still turn out in the thousands to hear Ralph Nader speak at campuses being attracted by

Lieberman's approach. Voter turnout among young people is at an all-time low, around 28 percent; and according to Voter News Service, while Bill Clinton had a 12-percentage-point margin over George H.W. Bush among 18–29 year olds in 1992 and a 19-percentage-point margin in 1996 Al Gore-Lieberman won this demographic by a mere 2 percent in 2000. None of the published postelection analyses by Democrats have focused on restoring turnout or Democratic margins among young voters.

Condescending to, alienating and demeaning young people is bad morally and bad politically. No progressive movement has ever succeeded without young people. Continued culture-bashing by Democrats opens the door for more erosion of their natural base to culture-savvy libertarians like Jesse Ventura.

> "*It is time to seriously consider the prospects for a universal rating system that could be applied across all media.*"

A Universal Ratings System Will Help Parents Monitor Media Violence

Dale Kunkel

Ratings are a tool parents can use to protect their children from media violence, which research shows is harmful, contends Dale Kunkel in the following viewpoint. However, claims Kunkel, parents have become so confused by the various age and content ratings among the different media that they do not use these ratings effectively. According to Kunkel, a universal ratings system across the media would help parents identify harmful content and protect their children from it. Kunkel is a professor of communications at University of California, Santa Barbara.

As you read, consider the following questions:
1. What examples does Kunkel provide to prove his assertion that parents are confused about the meaning of rating categories?
2. What obvious economic incentive does the author claim motivates television networks to rate programs leniently?
3. To what other uniform system employed by the government does Kunkel compare his concept of a universal media ratings system?

Dale Kunkel, testimony before the Senate Committee on Government Affairs, July 25, 2001.

I have conducted numerous studies over the past 15 years on the issues of media violence and sexual content, and served as a senior researcher from 1994–1998 on the National Television Violence Study, one of the largest media research projects as of July 25, 2001. I have also followed the topic of media ratings closely since the introduction of the V-chip which Congress triggered with an amendment to the Telecommunications Act of 1996. . . .

Why Media Ratings?

Concern on the part of the public and Congress about the harmful influence of media violence and other sensitive material on children dates back to the 1950s and 1960s. The legitimacy of that concern is corroborated by extensive scientific research that has accumulated since that time. Indeed, in reviewing the totality of empirical evidence regarding the impact of media violence, the conclusion that exposure to violent portrayals poses a risk of harmful effects on children has been reached by the U.S. Surgeon General, the National Institutes of Mental Health, the National Academy of Sciences, the American Medical Association, the American Psychological Association, the American Academy of Pediatrics, and a host of other scientific and public health agencies and organizations.

Lest I seem pedantic in reviewing this overwhelming consensus about the harmful effects of media violence, I must note a troubling development that has surfaced. Echoing patterns from the distant past, industry officials are once again contesting the premise that media violence poses a risk of harm for children. Indeed, in a letter written by Jack Valenti, Chairman of the Motion Picture Association, to Dr. David Walsh, President of the National Institute on Media and the Family, Mr. Valenti claims that the scientific community does not agree on the conclusions of research in this area. Mr. Valenti cites a research review funded by the Motion Picture Association that calls the evidence in this realm "inconsistent and weak." This stance sharply diverges from the position of industry leaders during the period in 1995–96 when the Congress was considering more stringent measures to address the problem of media violence. At that time, industry officials including Mr. Valenti were uniform in their recognition that media violence is a legitimate cause for concern, and they were quick to accept the V-chip rating system as an appropriate mechanism to address that concern in lieu of other policy options under consideration at the time that the industry found less palatable.

Notwithstanding Mr. Valenti's comments, it is well established by a compelling body of scientific evidence that television violence poses a risk of harmful effects for child-viewers. While exposure to media violence is not necessarily the most potent factor contributing to real world violence and aggression in the United States today, it is certainly the most pervasive. Millions of children spend an average of approximately 20 hours per week watching television, and this cumulative exposure to violent images can shape young minds in unhealthy ways.

Using media ratings as a means to address the problem of violence and other sensitive material in the media has both advantages and disadvantages. By merely labeling rather than limiting the presentation of material likely to be harmful to children, the rights of adults to watch whatever they choose are protected. But there are two important issues involving the use of media ratings to reduce children's exposure to violence and other types of potentially harmful content. One is the concern that parents may not understand and use the rating systems to help guide their children's media use; and the other is that media content may not be accurately labeled, resulting in inappropriate content "slipping through the cracks" in the filtering system of the V-chip and other rating formats even though parents actively employ them. These are the two key issues to consider in evaluating how well the current rating systems are working.

How Well Are Media Ratings Working?

Studies that examine parents' knowledge about and use of the V-chip television rating system have produced mixed results. Research conducted by both the Kaiser Family Foundation and the Annenberg Public Policy Center indicate that although a substantial proportion of parents know about the ratings, there is a lot of confusion about the meaning of the various categories and labels. This may account for why only a modest proportion of parents report using the ratings to make decisions about what their children may watch.

In May of 1999, the Kaiser Foundation reported that 77% of parents said they would use the V-chip if they had one. But the same study also found that only 44% of parents "often" or "sometimes" used the TV ratings to help guide their children's viewing. More recent research by the Annenberg Public Policy Center indicated that only about 50% of parents were aware of the V-chip ratings in 2000, compared to 70% in 1997 when the press coverage for the roll-out of the new system was at its peak. This reduction in the awareness of ratings almost certainly stems from the lack of any systematic effort by the television industry to publicize their ratings framework.

Even among those parents who know about the rating system, nine out of ten could not accurately identify the age ratings for a sample of programs their children watched, according to the Annenberg Center data. Confusion abounds about the meaning of many categories. For example, most parents mistakenly believe that the "FV" designation, which indicates "fantasy violence" in children's shows, is meant to identify programs appropriate for "family viewing." Given this confusion *within* the V-chip rating system itself, it is hardly surprising that the lack of consistency *across* the rating systems used for differing media—including films, television, music, and video games—leads to even more consternation on the part of parents trying to figure it all out.

Are Labels Accurate?

The second key issue to consider in assessing the efficacy of media ratings is whether or not the content that poses the greatest risk of harm to children is labeled accurately. If it is not, even those parents who understand and use the rating systems will not reap any benefits in reducing their children's exposure to potentially harmful material. In this realm, there are a number of concerns. Research I have conducted in the first and second years following adoption of the V-chip rating system indicated that the age-based rating judgments (TV-G, TV-PG, TV-14, etc.) were being applied accurately, but that the content-based descriptors (V for violence, S for sex, etc.) were not. Indeed, the majority of programs that contained violence did not receive a "V" rating and thus any parent using the V-chip to screen out programs rated with a "V" would accomplish little in reducing their children's exposure to television violence. If this pattern persists today, parents could not effectively screen out violent portrayals by relying upon the content-based aspect of the V-chip rating system.

A Need for an External Rating Board

From their inception in the movie industry, ratings have been implemented on a voluntary basis. The combination of industry and public pressures to use ratings has encouraged the makers of media products to use the ratings to label their products. In recent years, however, the economic stakes seem to have changed. The competition for the public's eye and wallet has sharpened considerably. The economic temptations to down rate a product to capture a larger audience have increased, and, at the same time, each passing season encourages producers to outdo the previous season in edgy material—with more violence, more sexual situations, and more adult language. The time has come for ratings to move beyond the voluntary arena. An external rating board with authority to assign and/or approve ratings grows increasingly necessary each year.

David A. Walsh and Douglas A. Gentile, *Pediatrics*, June 2001.

A recent study by researchers at the National Institute on Media and the Family published in the June 2001 issue of *Pediatrics* found that parents tend to rate programs in more restrictive fashion than the judgments that are applied to the same shows by the television industry. Given the obvious economic incentive for television networks to rate programs leniently so as to avoid diminishing their audience and hence reducing their revenue stream, this is a worrisome finding.

Finally, one additional concern involves limitations in the design of the rating categories rather than their application to specific shows. Children's programs may receive only one of two basic rating labels—either TV-Y, appropriate for all youth; or TV-Y7, appropriate for children age 7 and over. In many children's programs, there are significant amounts of violence that are presented in a manner that makes them particularly likely to encourage aggression and other harmful effects in child-viewers. For example, an episode of the futuristic cartoon "Beast Wars" showed hunters hovering in a helicopter, shooting wildlife below on the ground while exclaiming cheerfully "I love it when prey cannot shoot back!" The fact that such programs are rated as "fit" for those over age 7 strikes me as a fundamental design flaw in the current rating system, when clearly there are many children's shows on television that are inappropriate for those in the 7–10 year old range due to their violent content. This structural limitation of the current V-chip system is an independent issue from the question of how accurately the ratings are applied to most programs primarily intended for adult audiences.

How Can Media Ratings Be Improved?

The assignment of media ratings are determined by those in the industry who are responsible for the content's production and/or distribution. Practically speaking, there is probably no alternative to that course given the amount of material that must be categorized and the turn-around time constraints inherent in the rating process. Nonetheless, there is a rich body of scientific research that helps to identify the types of media content that pose the greatest risk of harmful effects on children. More training, education, or sensitivity on the part of raters to the relevant research about media effects on children is needed. This goal could be accomplished in a number of ways involving the cooperation of experts in the areas of child development, media effects, and the public health community. Unless media ratings can consistently and accurately label the content that poses the greatest risk of harm to children, such systems cannot accomplish much help for parents.

More active monitoring and oversight of the ratings process is also needed. While several of the media rating systems maintain advisory boards charged with supervisory responsibility, none have played a vigorous role in discharging their responsibilities to date, and all are dominated by media industry officials with only token participation at best by a parent or child advocate representative. There is a precedent for the television industry funding truly independent research from neutral parties to evaluate its performance in the realm of presenting violence responsibly, as was done with the National Television Violence Study and the UCLA Violence Report in the 1990s. Such an effort should be considered to evaluate the accuracy and consistency of rating judgments for the V-chip system as well as for other media rating systems.

A Universal Rating System

Finally, it is time to seriously consider the prospects for a universal rating system that could be applied across all media. The lack of consistency across media in their rating formats makes it incredibly difficult for parents to master all of the subtleties that vary across television ratings, film ratings, video games, and so on. As Dr. David Walsh has noted in a letter to the Senate Committee on Commerce, Science, and Transportation, a media product that included extreme violence would be rated R if it were a movie, TV-MA if it were a TV show, M if it were a home video game, display a red sticker if it were an arcade video game, or have a "Parental Advisory" sticker if it were a music CD. This causes needless confusion for parents, and undercuts the utility of all rating systems.

An apt comparison in this regard involves the uniform system of food labeling that is employed in the U.S. A consistent framework that indicates calories, grams of fat, and so on is included on all food packaging, and the uniformity of the system facilitates easy comparison across all types of food products. Imagine that food labeling was not accomplished uniformly, but rather in idiosyncratic fashion that made comparisons across different products impractical. Such a labeling system would be of little value to consumers—and that is the current situation we face with the alphabet soup of differing media rating systems.

I have already read the comments of media officials who claim "it can't be done" when the prospect of a uniform rating system is raised, but this appears to be little more than a knee-jerk reaction. The "can't be done" chorus was also heard when the V-chip idea first surfaced, but we have obviously proven that reaction wrong already. The potential value to parents of a uniform rating system is too great to pass up without serious consideration by all of the media industries. That consideration will not come without strong prompting from the public, and hearings such as this are an important catalyst to help focus the attention of already busy and overwhelmed parents on the importance of media in their children's lives. I commend this committee for its pursuit of this issue and its contribution to the ongoing public dialogue about the efficacy of media ratings.

"Not only would compulsory ratings violate the spirit of the First Amendment— quashing lively discussion in favor of fiat-by-label—they also violate its letter."

A Universal Ratings System Violates the First Amendment

Julie Hilden

A compulsory universal ratings system would violate the First Amendment, argues Julie Hilden in the following viewpoint. Hilden maintains that a universal rating system would censure otherwise worthwhile products by labeling them "violent." Moreover, claims Hilden, universal ratings violate the First Amendment because they force the media—by compelling them to apply negative labels to their works—to involuntarily speak against themselves. An attorney, Hilden represented media asserting First Amendment defenses and is now a freelance writer.

As you read, consider the following questions:
1. According to Hilden, why do ratings appear harmless to many Americans?
2. How do private ratings support the aims of the First Amendment, in the author's view?
3. In Hilden's opinion, why is compulsory speech that attacks one's own beliefs among the harshest of constitutional injuries?

Julie Hilden, "Hollywood-Bashing and the First Amendment," *FindLaw's Writ*, September 21, 2000. Copyright © 2000 by FindLaw. This column was originally published on FindLaw.com. Reproduced by permission.

Across the political spectrum in the fall of 2001, it's "Burn, Hollywood, Burn." An issue that might have divided the parties—whether and how to regulate "violent" movies—has them trampling one another in their race to leap onto the bandwagon. The issue is not whether to hate Hollywood, but rather, who hates Hollywood most.

Is it [music label] sticker mom Tipper Gore, Silver Sewer [an award identifying alleged cultural polluters], innovator Joe Lieberman, or *Crossfire* complainer Lynn Cheney? Is it Al Gore, who's threatened to unleash the Federal Trade Commission (FTC) and let it regulate movie studios as if they were tobacco companies?

Or is it the average American? It may well be. According to a poll by Mark Penn, only about fifteen percent of the American public believes the First Amendment protects Hollywood movies from any government action. More incredibly, twenty-two percent of the public supports government content restrictions on movies that would, if enacted, constitute blatant constitutional violations.

Recalling that one of the First Amendment's purposes is to protect unpopular speech, one may wonder how the Amendment itself became so unpopular. When did we stop believing in the First Amendment, when it comes to regulating movie violence, and why?

Violence Ratings Are Everywhere

One reason the public doesn't worry about protecting the First Amendment from movie violence regulation may be that the most common panacea offered is a government ratings system. Since ratings are already ubiquitous, more ratings appear harmless. On the Internet movie reviews, "grades" and evaluations of suitability for children are widely available. *Slate, moviefone.com* and *Entertainment Weekly* even offer buffets of different critics' ratings from which to choose.

As a result, the compulsory "universal ratings system" proposed by some may seem to be one more innocuous consumer service: the government's variant of what is already available from private companies. And Hollywood's complaints about such a system may seem as whiny as complaints about unfavorable reviews. But as a matter of both constitutional law and real-world practice, making voluntary ratings compulsory would transform them profoundly—from a service to a threat.

The spectrum of voluntary ratings and reviews that is now available vindicates the First Amendment's concept of a "marketplace of ideas" from which to choose. On the Internet and in print, the overwhelming majority of ratings or grades are connected to a review that is, at most, a click away. And of course, by reading a critic's review, we can also divine his point of view. Even if we only consult ratings, we have a choice among many; if we see that a movie received the equivalent of a C from critics, we can also see, in one of the "review buffets," that moviegoers gave it an A. One critic may find a movie unsuitable for children because it contains violence; another might find it virtually obligatory for them because it shows violence's toll.

Whose Values Do Ratings Reflect?

Maybe we are asking ratings to do too much. Ratings are value judgments, not objective scientific standards; but whose values do they reflect? Hollywood's 1930 Production Code, which regulated movie content for three decades, was authored in the context of a threatened boycott of American cinema by the Legion of Decency and other conservative Christian groups. Although its standards still influence our current ratings system, the code never reflected a national consensus—and in any case, a unified set of value judgments makes increasingly less sense within an ever more multicultural society.

Henry Jenkins, *Technology Review*, November 2001.

In short, private ratings generally shore up the aims of the First Amendment, in that they are diverse, transparent and well-explained. Compulsory ratings, on the other hand, would be anti-First Amendment, in that they are likely to be univocal, opaque and explained only by a label or a few conclusory words. Of course, this last point might also be made about the current voluntary movie rating system—which also provides ratings without reviews. But the current system's language, a dry assessment of age-appropriateness, does not condemn and deprecate as strongly as the proposed systems of violence-assessment would. Such a rating system, especially with the aegis of the government behind it, would be very much like a blacklist—which tries to taint by naming, without fully explaining.

Just as being named on a blacklist can dehumanize a person by reducing him to "a Communist," so too can an unexplained or partially-explained rating dehumanize a movie—reducing it to "a violent film." *The Basketball Diaries*, for example—a worthwhile movie the message of which actually favored recovery from drugs and violence—has now been reduced to the image of Leonardo DiCaprio with a gun in a long black coat, and deemed "a violent movie." This is akin to reducing *The Scarlet Letter* to the image of Hester Prynne having sex with the Reverend Dimmesdale, and calling it "an adulterous book."

What's So Bad About a Little Box in Your Ads?

Not only would compulsory ratings violate the spirit of the First Amendment—quashing lively discussion in favor of fiat-by-label—they also violate its letter. One important aspect of the First Amendment is the right not to be forced to voice the opinions of others, including those of the government.

Accordingly, the Supreme Court has held that one cannot be forced, for example, to salute the flag, to take a loyalty oath with which one disagrees—or even to display on one's license plate a state motto contrary to one's own beliefs, thus becoming the motto's moving billboard. But a government-rated movie is exactly that—a moving billboard for the government's message.

Compulsory speech that attacks one's own beliefs is among the harshest of constitutional injuries. Being forced to swear loyalty smacks of fascism. Being forced to renounce one's own beliefs, and admit you were wrong, is what is done in the torture room. Yet compulsory movie ratings that force a studio, writers and actors who believe in a movie nevertheless to label it "violent" or "unsuitable for children" don't seem to bother us. Why? Is it because of the heights of self-flagellation to which we've driven tobacco companies, starting with boxed Surgeon General's warnings, and culminating in powerful anti-youth-smoking ads?

This level of self-flagellation may be proper for an industry with a product that kills; and that juries have found have lied about that fact to the public for years. But unlike tobacco, movies—even violent ones—aren't inherently bad; on the contrary, they are just as likely to enrich and enable a healthy culture as to destroy one. (*Saving Private Ryan? Apocalypse Now?*) Nor have movie industry executives ever been found to have lied to the public.

But What About the Children?

So far, that is. The FTC is now trying to catch the movie industry in supposed "lies"—or at least in hypocrisy—by suggesting that the industry markets R-rated movies to children. The FTC is trying to hit the industry where it's weak—advertising traditionally has received less constitutional protection than other speech, and who wants to argue against protecting children? The sense that "It's only ads," or "It's for the *kids*," may be animating our recent complacency. But this attack is deeply unfair.

Reportedly, the FTC has evidence of a studio using eleven-year-olds as a focus group for an R movie. Is this such a great transgression? I probably saw my first R-rated movie when I was around twelve, and I'm not in jail yet. The same is true for many Americans. The focus group kids must have had parental permission. And kids can see R-rated movies if their parents accompany them. Or have we forgotten the difference between R and X ratings? Finally, if kids are going to lobby their parents to allow particular R-rated movies, then it seems fine for the industry to market those movies to them; after all, they are part of the target audience. Only a campaign to inspire kids to sneak into R-rated movies over their parents' objections would be truly hypocritical.

And even if you disagree with everything I've said about the focus groups, the solution is not to impose a compulsory ratings system. It is merely to stop focus groups from using minors. A few anecdotes should not serve as a wedge for much more expansive regulation. That's what the FTC may be hoping for. But that's not what the public—cognizant of the First Amendment—should allow.

"Events portrayed on television news have generated copycat crimes."

The Government Should Restrict News Coverage of Violent Crime

Paul Klite

The violent crime coverage that dominates television news is part of the culture of violence that threatens society, argues Paul Klite in the following viewpoint. Violent crime coverage has both short- and long-term negative effects, claims Klite, from generating copycat crimes to making people numb to violence. Unfortunately, Klite contends, because violence creates the arousal that sells merchandise, advertisers support news programs that show violence. Klite, who died on June 24, 2000, was executive director of Rocky Mountain Media Watch, a media watchdog organization.

As you read, consider the following questions:

1. According to Klite, what percentage of time do TV newscasts devote to violent topics?
2. In the author's opinion, what are the long-term effects of exposure to violent news images?
3. What does the author suggest will break the cycle of exploitive violence?

In the aftermath of the Columbine High School tragedy in Littleton, Colorado, a broad national debate has developed to intervene in the American "culture of violence." Many fingerprints are on the proverbial trigger—inadequate parenting; the availability of guns; alienation of youth; mental illness, school security, manipulative violence in film, video games, television, the internet and pop music.

Let us also include the contribution of television news to this toxic stew. More than society's messenger, more than a mirror of reality, the electronic communication media collect and concentrate the planet's woes and deliver them into our living rooms each night. The seventy-five percent of Americans who watch TV news regularly are subjected to a substantial nightly dose of catastrophe. And, in the news, the blood is real.

Journalists by now know that their broadcast images have enormous power and must be handled with sensitivity. Yet, the news industry has no ethical guidelines for airing violent images.

The Dangers of News Violence

Events portrayed on television news have generated copycat crimes, including mass murder, terrorism, hijackings, workplace violence, product tampering, hate crimes and suicide. Following the Littleton terrorism, hundreds of acts of mimicry have been reported across the U.S. The succession of school killings are themselves examples of copycat events. The widespread publicity that followed similar crimes in other locales provides a relentless supply of examples of how to conduct assault operations on schools. The notoriety perpetrators receive can itself be a motivator for others to imitate violent acts.

Numerous research studies over the last three decades have reported that viewing violent video teaches violent resolution of conflict, encourages aggressive behavior and diminishes empathy for victims. With the average weekly dose of TV in the U.S. at 20 to 30 hours, these effects are reinforced through repetition. The Surgeon General, American Medical Association, American Academy of Pediatrics, American Psychoanalytical Association and the National PTA have all warned about these phenomena.

Analysis of local TV newscasts across the country over the last five years by Rocky Mountain Media Watch document that violent topics consistently comprise 40 to 50 percent of all the air-time devoted to news. Crime rates are down across the U.S., but not on local TV news. Murder, one of the least common crimes committed, is the number one topic on newscasts.

The "Mean-World" Syndrome

Viewers develop what [George] Gerbner calls the *"mean-world syndrome."* People who often watch this violence believe that the world is a more dangerous place than it really is. With the mean-world syndrome, heavy viewers change their views about violence.

- In the long term, they begin to see violence as the solution to almost any problem.

- They become accustomed to violence. They are numbed to the brutality.

- They develop a sense of fear and danger. *"There's a mistrust of strangers who look or act differently."*

David A. Gershaw, "A Line on Life: News Media and the Mean World," April 21, 1996.

TV sells what it shows, be it hair-raising medicine or hair-raising mayhem. By repetition, gruesome images have been burned into our brains just like images of heavily advertised products. Television's power to influence behavior and belief attracts billions of advertising dollars yearly. Cultural habits and values are also susceptible to television's influence and TV news images can drag us into wars, out of wars and elect our leaders.

Long term, we get "used to it." Numbness and cynicism replace fear, terror and revulsion. The effects are cumulative, producing what George Gerbner calls the "Mean World Syndrome," where viewers perceive the world as a more fearful place than it actually is. Each exposure to media violence becomes a one part-per-billion dose of more alienation. Millions are afraid to go out at night, do not trust their neighbors and feel estranged from society in proportion to their media exposure.

Challenging Media Supporters

Some insist that media violence is harmless entertainment, escapist fare or cathartic diversion, or that people have a "taste for violence." Others, desensitized by hundreds of thousands of acts of violence they have seen on TV, deny the problem. Industry moguls bristle at any talk of regulating their bread-and-butter fare of mayhem, and reject the evidence of its harmful effects. Their views are self-serving and must be challenged.

A word rarely mentioned in this debate is sadism, broadly defined as the enjoyment of others' pain. Is that not what we are doing when we relish watching violent news, entertainment and sports? That violent media attracts mass audiences suggests we may be nurturing a culture of sadism.

Violence attracts people's attention and produces a strong emotional reaction that advertisers covet. Marketeers call it arousal. Paraphrasing Marshall McLuhan, arousal helps move merchandise. Violence, talk of violence and threat of violence are the most effective tools for manipulating people—propagandists from Machiavelli to Mao have known this. Like an addictive drug, we have been subjected to ever increasing doses of more and more graphic violence over the last few decades.

What can be done? One, lower the dose of news violence and, as Max Frankel suggests, explain the cruelty, don't just film it. In real life, violence has consequences. Balanced news includes a balance of topics. Two, educate broadcasters about their power for harm and have the industry develop ethical standards for dealing with potentially hazardous material. Three, require warning labels directly on television broadcasts in the form of prime-time public service announcements that explain and alert viewers to harmful TV effects. The cycle of exploitive violence on the news must be broken.

"I can't think of anything worse or more horrifying than the idea of asking the FCC to serve as the national nanny of the quality of the news."

The Government Should Not Restrict News Coverage of Violent Crime

Lawrence K. Grossman

Asking the federal government to restrict excessive news coverage of violent crime is unconstitutional, argues Lawrence K. Grossman in the following viewpoint. Although Grossman agrees that coverage of violent crime is excessive, the responsibility for improving local television news, he maintains, should not rest with the government but with consumers. Grossman is a former president of NBC News and the Public Broadcasting System.

As you read, consider the following questions:
1. According to Grossman, from whom did Paul Klite get encouragement and advice?
2. In Grossman's opinion, why did the FCC have a valid interest in the challenge he made against a New York City television station?
3. Short of government intervention, what can be done to improve local TV news, in Grossman's view?

Lawrence K. Grossman, "Does Local TV News Need a National Nanny?" *Columbia Journalism Review*, vol. 35, May/June, 1998, p. 33. Copyright © 1998 by Columbia University, Graduate School of Journalism. Reproduced by permission.

L ord, save us from the saviors. In a dramatic, highly publicized move to reform local TV news, Rocky Mountain
Media Watch, a Denver-based nonprofit group, has peti-
tioned the Federal Communications Commission [FCC] to
deny the licenses of four hometown TV stations, KWGN,
KCNC, KMGH, and KUSA. Media Watch calls the stations' local newscasts "toxic" to Denver citizens.

Its unprecedented filing also asks the FCC to require the
stations to air public service announcements confessing their
"unbalanced and unhealthy diet of information and its potentially harmful side-effects"; run daily prime time programs teaching "media literacy"; give mandatory education
and training to their news staffs; and draw up plans to improve local election coverage.

Analyzing the Local News

Since 1994, Media Watch has been analyzing the nation's local TV news shows and finding them (surprise! surprise!) full
of murder, mayhem, fluff, chit-chat, over-commercialization,
and racial and gender stereotyping. Media Watch's lone paid
staff member, executive director Paul Klite, is a former public radio talk show host, producer, and medical doctor who
knows how to attract attention. Support for his group comes
from some 200 contributors and a few local foundations and
200 volunteers who send in tapes of the shows Media Watch
watches. Asked who does the content analysis, Klite says he
does, along with three volunteers, one of whom is a Ph.D.
mathematician; the other two he describes as public-interest
activists.

Klite says he got encouragement and advice for his FCC
action from Ralph Nader [a consumer advocate and Green
party presidential candidate], former FCC Commissioner
Nicholas Johnson, and University of Pennsylvania media
guru George Gerbner—all of whom should know better
than to invite in government agents to monitor TV news
content. His real purpose in filing the petition, he says, was
"to get people's attention." He's gotten plenty of it in Denver, in trade publications, and throughout the country. The
Boston Globe played the story on page one.

Of course, asking the FCC, a politically appointed agency,

The Public Demands Crime Reportage

News editors and producers are not generating . . . coverage
[of murders] due to some ideological agenda of their own;
they are doing it because, in their drive to augment audience
sizes, they must act on their strong intuitions that the public
demands such reportage. Because there is little resistance
and no backlash from viewers and readers regarding crime
stories, it appears likely that the editors are correct. A conclusion is that the public, entering into a strongly fearful and
repressive period, wants stories that articulate its anxieties.

Jib Fowles, *The Case for Television Violence*, 1999.

to serve as local censor and news editor happens to violate
the Communications Act (section 326) as well as the Constitution (the First Amendment). So the FCC should, and undoubtedly will, throw out the Media Watch petition with all
undeliberate speed.[1] I say that even though . . . in 1968 I organized a citizens' group to challenge the license of WPIX,
a New York City station owned by the *Chicago Tribune* and
the *New York Daily News*. We charged the station with gross
failure to serve the needs and interests of the New York
metropolitan area and with purposely falsifying and distort-
ing its news reports. Among other egregious news practices,
the station labeled old stock footage as on-the-scene reports
of citizen protests in Eastern Europe, described army publicity film shot in Fort Belvoir, Virginia, as coming "via
satellite from the Central Highlands of Vietnam," and identified audio reports called in from a pay phone on Forty-sec-
ond street as "live from Prague." When members of WPIX's
news staff complained about having to falsify the news, they
were fired. But those charges involved factual issues of deliberate news falsification and distortion by a station li-
censee, in which the FCC has a valid interest. (After years of
hearings, WPIX promised to reform, replaced its general
manager and news director, settled with the challengers, and
retained its license.)

Media Watch denies that its FCC petition against the
Denver stations involves censorship. "No one," it says, "wants
the government to regulate news content or interfere with

1. The FCC renewed the stations' licenses in April 1998.

broadcasters' First Amendment guarantees." The petition depicts the problem as really "a public health issue" of "toxic television news" that goes "beyond bad journalism." Perhaps Dr. Klite should have directed his filing to the U.S. Surgeon General.

The Case Against TV News

The assertion of Media Watch that local TV news across the nation tends to be "severely unbalanced, with excessive coverage of violent topics and trivial events" jibes with just about every other study. . . . [In 1997] The *Detroit News* reported that in the Motor City, "Crime and violence constitute by far the largest share of the coverage," taking up an average of 43 percent of all newscasts. The nonpartisan Center for Media and Public Affairs in Washington, D.C., recently analyzed three months of nightly local news in thirteen cities and also found that crime dominated. Crime, weather, accidents, disasters, soft news, and sports accounted for the majority of stories on the newscasts the center studied. Add in time for credits and commercials, the center noted, and you get a total of 24 minutes and 20 seconds per half-hour newscast— and that leaves just five minutes and forty seconds to cover all other "serious news" about government, health, foreign affairs, education, science, the environment . . .

Notwithstanding the fact that local TV news is generally awful throughout the nation, former FCC General Counsel Henry Geller's reaction to the Rocky Mountain petition is right on target: "I can't think of anything worse or more horrifying than the idea of asking the FCC to serve as the national nanny of the quality of the news."

Can anything short of government intervention be done to improve local TV news? It's an uphill battle. The way to fight is to keep up the barrage of healthy public criticism; organize expressions of outrage by concerned journalists and boycotts by irate viewers; expose the miscreants who do the most atrocious news job (but make sure to expose the right miscreants), and mount as much peer pressure as possible.

But at all costs, keep the government out of the newsroom.

Periodical Bibliography

The following articles have been selected to supplement the diverse views presented in this chapter.

Paige Albiniak   "Washington Demands," *Broadcasting & Cable*, May 17, 1999.

Kris Axtman   "Media Violence May Be Easier Tarred than Regulated," *Christian Science Monitor*, September 14, 2000.

Peter Calcagno   "V-Chip Parenting," *Ludwig von Mises Institute*, June 10, 1999. www.mises.org.

Doreen Carvajal   "Major Studios Used Children to Test-Market Violent Films," *New York Times*, September 27, 2000.

Gina R. Dalfonzo   "Good Old-Fashioned Shame," *Family Research Council*, 2002. www.frc.org.

Roger Donway   "Support the Media's Right to Be Disgusting," *Navigator*, February 2001.

Faye Fiore   "Movie Executives Offer to Curb Some Marketing to Kids," *Los Angeles Times*, September 28, 2000.

Sonya A. Grier   "The Federal Trade Commission's Report on the Marketing of Violent Entertainment to Youths: Developing Policy-Tuned Research," *Journal of Public Policy & Marketing*, Spring 2001.

Lynette Holloway   "Music Industry Is Resisting Tougher Label Standards," *New York Times*, October 21, 2002.

Wendy Kaminer   "Toxic Media," *American Prospect*, October 23, 2000.

David E. Rosenbaum   "Violence on the Screen: Unlovely and Invulnerable," *New York Times*, September 24, 2000.

Ronald D. Rotunda   "The FTC Report on Hollywood Entertainment," *Federalist Society*, September 15, 2000. www.fedsoc.org.

Michael Schneider   "Bored Lips Sink Chips: After All the Fuss, Net Content Is Relegated to Back Burner," *Variety*, December 17, 2001.

Christopher Stern   "D.C. Thrusts, H'wood Parries," *Variety*, May 10, 1999.

Phillip Taylor   "Senator Defends Entertainment-Labeling Bill as 'Citizenship,' Not Censorship," www.freedomforum.org, September 3, 1999.

CHAPTER 3

How Should Society Respond to Media Violence?

Chapter Preface

The quantity of media technology found in American homes has increased substantially in the last decade and, as a consequence, so has the amount of violent content to which children are exposed. According to a study conducted by the Henry J. Kaiser Foundation, the average American child grows up in a home with three televisions, three tape players, three radios, two CD players, two VCRs, one video game player, and one computer. In 1998, 38 percent of homes had Internet access; in 2001 that percentage had increased to 69. Opinions on the impact of media technology in the home and, more particularly, the affect of increased exposure to violent media content on children, vary significantly. People also disagree on exactly how society should respond to media violence, if at all.

One of several ways commentators recommend society respond to media violence is to create a healthy media environment within the home. According to some childhood development experts, the problem is not simply what children see, but where they see it. The choices individual families make, such as where to put the family computer or video game console and how many television sets a household has, can influence the impact of these technologies, analysts claim. Of children between eight and eighteen, 65 percent have a television in their bedroom, 45 percent have a video game player, and 75 percent a CD player. Children's bedrooms have become what some deem "media central." According to William Damon, director of the Stanford University Center on Adolescence, when these media technologies move into children's rooms, "the whole pattern of use of mass media works to isolate children from adults." Parents can urge children to question media images, but only if they know what is on the screen. The American Academy of Pediatrics therefore recommends in its report on media education that parents should create an electronic media-free environment in all children's rooms.

Parents employ different strategies to control their children's media environment in the home. The Warrens, a family who live in Brookville, an affluent community on Long Island have placed three computers in the playroom to be used by their three children. The family uses an Internet service provider that allows parents to control where their children can go on the Internet by choosing browser settings that prevent access to sites determined to be unsuitable for children. They have chosen to use these settings as a disciplinary tool for their teenage daughter. While her Internet access is generally unrestricted, when she misbehaves, her parents limit her access to "mature teen." In addition, although the Warrens want to give their children privacy and allow them to have their own passwords, Ms. Warren occasionally checks the computer's history files to monitor where her children have been on the Internet.

This strategy does not work for all parents because many are not as computer savvy as the Warrens nor do they have the time to monitor their children's use of media. For example, unlike Ms. Warren, who is a stay-at-home mother, Joselyn Fernandez, a single mother from New York City's rough West Harlem neighborhood, is raising two sons while working at night and going to nursing school during the day. Her older son often cocoons himself away in the bedroom he shares with his brother and grandfather playing high-carnage video games and listening to rap music. Ms. Fernandez is less troubled by the violence in her son's entertainments, however, than she is by the world outside her door. When his friends come over to play video games in her son's room, she reasons, they are safer than if they were out on the streets. She feels that if she removed all of the media technology from her son's room, the safe haven would become less attractive to her son and his friends, and they would probably spend less time there and more time on the streets.

People continue to debate whether and how parents should monitor their children's exposure to media violence. The viewpoints in the following chapter discuss this issue as well as other ways society might respond to the problem of violence in the media.

"Parents are in the best position to guide children in appropriate and healthy media use habits."

Parents Should Monitor Their Children's Media Habits

Marjorie J. Hogan

In the following viewpoint, Marjorie J. Hogan argues that parents are in the best position to monitor their children's media habits because parents know the needs of their own children better than anyone else. Hogan claims that parents have the authority to establish rules for media use that limit the quantity and control the quality of media exposure. By helping their children examine and question media images, she claims, parents can become the family's media educators. Hogan is director of pediatric medical education at Hennepin County Medical Center in Minneapolis, Minnesota.

As you read, consider the following questions:

1. What opportunities does Hogan claim could bring media education into the family conversation?
2. According to the author, how is eating healthy foods analogous to consuming a healthy media diet?
3. In Hogan's opinion, in what ways do parents benefit from coviewing programs and using media products with their children?

P arents and other caregivers of children and adolescents, whether grandparents, foster parents, community elders, or other adults in a parental role, are the most important models, monitors, and mediators of appropriate media use for children and adolescents. In our rapidly evolving modern society, churches and communities no longer are able or expected to be traditional cultural teachers for youth; the homogenized picture of American culture is provided through characters, plots, and commercials on screens and other media across the land. Years ago, respected researcher George Gerbner noted that our common cultural teacher was entertainment television, "a set of cultural indicators—symbolic representations of the power relations and human values of our culture."

Media messages and images are ubiquitous and penetrate deeply into the lives of young people. In the United States, 87% of families have more than one television set per household, and 46% of homes own all four electronic media—television, VCR, video game player, and computer. In 1999, 41% of families were on-line, and 48% of children boasted a television set in their bedroom. Children 2 through 17 years of age spend an average of 4.35 hours per day in front of a screen (TV, videotape, computer, or video game). Whereas children and adolescents spend an average of 2.46 hours watching television every day, they spend an average of only 1.14 hours doing homework and 0.77 hours reading books.

The Importance of the Parental Role

Parents can incorporate the lessons from their own experience, values, cultural traditions, and spiritual beliefs into a unique parenting style, providing balance from the barrage of media messages encountered by children. In our diverse American society, families from vastly different cultures, countries, and circumstances struggle to make sense of our shared media as they influence their lives and their children.

In addition to being cultural teachers, parents know each individual child best. A parent understands the personality, the developmental path, and the special needs of a given child or adolescent. Children of different ages, distinctive temperaments, and diverse experience respond uniquely to media images and messages. For example, a preschool-age child who has recently lost an aging grandparent may be especially vulnerable to fears after watching a scary movie on videocassette. A child living in a neighborhood rife with real-life violence from gunfire will likely feel more frightened after seeing stories about death on the news or watching a prime-time, violent, made-for-TV movie. Young people with learning disabilities may become more distractible after any time spent watching a rapidly paced action show; homework, or any task requiring attention and organization, suffers. Many young children enjoy a rich, creative imagination; savvy parents know that such children may have heightened fears after exposure to media themes beyond their ken and control. Attuned parents provide guidance about and control over exposure to certain media offerings because they understand the strength and fragility unique to each child.

Parents are in a position to work with other partners invested in optimizing media for children and families. Many parents are integral members of PTA groups across the country and can set the agenda for these influential, local bodies. Parents and families form communities and, with collaboration and commitment, can generate neighborhood-based movements to sponsor "TV-Turnoff Weeks," alternative activities for children and adolescents, and letter-writing campaigns about good or bad media programs.

For compelling reasons, parents are in the best position to guide children in appropriate and healthy media use habits:

- Parents can be cultural teachers for children, understanding the importance of family priorities and beliefs and how media messages and images affect the family.
- Parents know and have empathy for their own children's strengths and vulnerabilities.
- Parents can partner with others (other parents, schools, and community groups) interested in optimizing media for children and in supporting media literacy in the classroom.
- Parents have the opportunity, through access and authority, to establish rules and guidance beginning in infancy and continuing through adolescence. . . .

The Effects of Media on Children

Parents and other advocates for children are becoming increasingly concerned about the potential negative impact of media. Understanding the existing research and experience regarding the effects of messages and images from various forms of media on children and adolescents reinforces the need for parental control and monitoring in the home. As Dr. Jerome Singer stated in the video program *On Television*,

> Parents have to realize that there is a stranger in your house. If you came home and you found a strange man . . . teaching your kids to punch each other, or trying to sell them all kinds of products, you'd kick him right out of the house. But here you are; you come in and the TV is on; and you don't think twice about it.

Sometimes the impact of media exposure on young viewers is immediate and unmistakable (e.g., when a preschooler imitates violent karate moves seen on a favorite cartoon show or when children clamor for a certain sweetened cereal advertised heavily on network television). Usually, the effects of media on children and adolescents are cumulative, akin to a slowly growing stalagmite in a cave; over time, with repeated exposure to the same messages and images, attitudes and behaviors change. . . .

Media Education Within the Family

The ubiquitous nature of media in our children's lives, and the potential harm from exposure to media messages and images, leads parents and other caregivers to turn to media education, or media literacy, as a simple and effective approach to managing media use in the home. More than schools, communities, or government mandates, parents are in a unique and powerful position to control, limit, and shape media use habits for their children through media education. . . .

For families, media education is the process of becoming selective, wise, and critical media consumers. Some of the components of media education, or media literacy, include the following:
- People create (construct) media messages.
- Each form of media uses its own language and techniques.

- No two people experience media messages in the same way.
- Each media message has its own values and point of view.

Parents can teach and model these insights for children and ensure that media education permeates every aspect of life in a family. Media education is a lifelong skill that will make all of us better media consumers, whether we are enjoying a movie, reading a newspaper, listening to a political ad, or surfing the Internet. Children who are media educated should enter adolescence and adulthood with a healthy cynicism about media offerings. Is this movie worth the price of admission? Do I believe this political candidate's pledges? Why are young women's bodies being used to promote this brand of beer?

Parents can and should use every opportunity to bring media education into the family conversation:

- Sitting around the dinner table discussing a newspaper article
- Planning to watch an educational TV show about Siberian tigers as a family
- Discussing a billboard advertising alcohol while driving to a family activity
- Coviewing a popular sitcom with young teens and their friends and "talking back" to the characters about their offensive dialogue

Media education, through filtering, questioning, and analyzing media images and messages, is fun and empowering for children and adults. Media education, when incorporated into everyday life, allows children to feel "smarter than the TV," savvy about advertising, and thus better able to evaluate products and be in control of misleading messages. Media education skills are also passed on between children; for example, if your child "talks back" to the TV about violence in a cartoon, this can have a powerful influence on a young friend visiting for the afternoon. When a child cries "Aha!" upon discovering the power of deconstructing a media message and passes that skill to family and friends, the potential "impact factor" of media education is realized.

Basic media education principles for the family are simple and effective:

- Arrange your home to be a positive media environment.
- Establish clear, fair rules about media use for your family.
- Encourage active, critical viewing of media programs amplified by family discussions. . . .

The Roles Parents Play

Keeping in mind the basic principles of media education, parents can play specific roles that work effectively within individual families. In becoming a media-educated (media-literate) family, flexibility, humor, and good communication are paramount. Media education is a process, and adults and children work together to optimize media use through the following guidelines.

Media Use in Children's Rooms

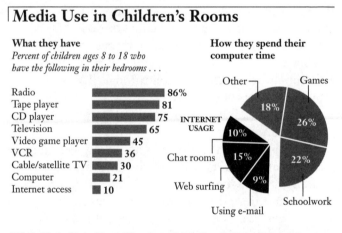

What they have
Percent of children ages 8 to 18 who have the following in their bedrooms . . .

Radio	86%
Tape player	81
CD player	75
Television	65
Video game player	45
VCR	36
Cable/satellite TV	30
Computer	21
Internet access	10

How they spend their computer time

Games 26%
Schoolwork 22%
Other 18%
INTERNET USAGE 10%
Chat rooms 15%
Web surfing 9%
Using e-mail

Kids & Media @ the New Millennium, Kaiser Family Foundation, November 1999.

For many years, the American Academy of Pediatrics (AAP) has recommended that children's and adolescents' media time be limited to 1 to 2 hours of quality programming daily. Each family, according to priorities, values, and interests, must define "quality." Time spent with any form of media, high quality or not, is time away from friends and family, active pursuits, creative play and hobbies, reading, and homework.

Media-educated parents and children can discuss establishing clear and consistent rules for media use, including finishing homework before watching TV or playing video games. Some families allow more flexibility with hours on weekends or during the summer, but well-enforced, respected limits on total screen time and on the kind of programs deemed appropriate are important bases of media education. Such limits are difficult to employ for the first time with an older child or adolescent; rules are best instituted and applied consistently when children are young. Parents should explain why specific media rules are instituted: "The violence in this program doesn't teach how to solve a problem"; "the language we hear on this program is very disrespectful to others"; or "there will be no video games until your homework is completed." This respectful approach to establishing guidelines for family media use teaches children and adolescents about parents' values and limits. . . .

Choosing Quality Programs

Whether television shows, films in the theater or on video, or computer software, choosing quality programs and products is an essential component of media education. Families should plan their media schedule actively and wisely. If a program of interest to the family (e.g., a sporting event or a special on animals) is scheduled during the week, this show should be a planned, anticipated family event. Family media plans should reflect each family's value system, and guidelines for content should take into account ages and interests of family members. Some families may like to catch a weekly baseball game on television, while others eagerly await a nature show on public television. Another family may allot one half-hour weekly for an anticipated family comedy series. The salient concept is the "media plan." . . .

Using a healthy diet as an analogy, as proposed in *The Smart Parent's Guide to Kids' TV*, parents decide which components of a "healthy media diet" will benefit their own children. Children and adolescents readily grasp this concept. We do not eat too many fat-laden foods because they are not good for our bodies and, similarly, too many violent or worthless programs are not conducive to healthy bodies and minds. Just as parents encourage healthy, nutrient-rich foods (although still in moderation), it is important to steer our children toward educational, positive media choices. . . .

As important as choosing appropriate programs and products, parents also may have to act as censors within the home, forbidding inappropriate programming. This could include the evening newscast, often featuring lurid or violent current events ("if it bleeds, it leads"); prime-time television shows; daytime "tell-all" television shows; or some music television.

More than 50% of adolescents under age 17 have attended popular R-rated movies. Movie theaters and managers are ill equipped to check the ages of all theater patrons, and many young people slip into inappropriate movies without parental consent. Others purchase tickets to PG or PG-13 movies and attend the R-rated feature instead. Still more bothersome, many parents bring young children to R-rated movies rife with violence, graphic sexual themes, and lurid language, perhaps not realizing the potential impact on the immature viewer. Choosing appropriate media content and programming for children and teens extends to the movie theater. Firm, consistent parental rules and optimal surveillance by theater workers are important measures.

Being a Positive Media Role Model

Parental roles of guiding children toward positive media choices and forbidding inappropriate media will help them to internalize the concept of choosing quality programs and products by themselves.

Children learn through imitation and reinforcement; media habits are no exception. If parents (the primary role models) hope to engender positive media habits in children, they must limit their own time in front of the screen and model preplanning and good choices in their lives. Parents who value active pursuits, love to read, enjoy time with friends and family, and tackle new hobbies with enthusiasm teach children far more powerful lessons than words ever could. . . .

Experiencing Media with Your Children

Research teaches us that coviewing, watching programs and using media products with your children, is a critical component of media education. Knowing what their children are watching allows parents to be involved in choices, to make priorities clear, and to encourage media literacy. A coviewing parent, through astute observations and questions about media messages, can make a poor program a learning experience, whereas a wonderful program watched by a child without a parent in attendance may be a wasted opportunity for learning and enjoyment. According to B.A. Eisenstock:

> Co-viewing, whether with a parent, other adult, sibling or peer, provides a critical opportunity to mediate children's understanding and interpretation of the reality and morality of messages, as well as their attitudes, values and knowledge about the world in which they live and the appropriate ways to act in the world.

Coviewing can
- Influence a child's judgment about the representation of TV characters
- Help children's understanding of plots and story lines
- Mediate potentially harmful effects of aggressive and violent content (when adult disapproval is expressed and discussion of nonviolent values is advanced). . . .

Understanding Current Ratings Systems

For many years, the age-based Motion Picture Association of America (MPAA) ratings system has been in place for movies produced in the United States, and parents, over the years, have become familiar with the meaning behind a G-, PG-, PG-13-, R-, or NC-17-rated film. This familiarity with the ratings does not imply that parents always agree with the ratings; in fact, studies have shown that a significant percentage of parents disagree. Many professional organizations, as well as parents, would still prefer a content-based ratings system for all forms of media.

In 1997, the television industry, under pressure from parents, advocacy groups, and some government leaders, instituted an age-based ratings system for many television programs. This system, reminiscent of the MPAA system for movies, allows producers to voluntarily rate their own shows.

With the advent of the highly touted V-chip, parents with this technology will be able to block certain undesirable programs in their homes. However, the rating system is far from ideal: News and sports programs are not rated; not all networks agreed to use the system; and the programs are still rated by a not-disinterested producer. Only the most intense level of content is displayed on the TV screen and determines the overall rating; content existing at lower levels is not displayed. In addition, the rating flashes on the screen at the beginning of the program and may be missed by parents.

Studies have shown that, for some children (particularly young boys), a mature rating, whether for television or movies, increases the young viewer's incentive to watch the show or movie—the "forbidden fruit" quandary. Ratings do not predict the appropriateness of a product or program for a particular child. These shortcomings underscore the important role parents play in mediating the media choices of children. Whether a television show or movie is rated G or higher, a parent knows the unique fears and sensitivities of a child or adolescent and should exercise the option of forbidding viewing of that program. Similarly, in some cases, a show with a prohibitive rating may be appropriate or educational at a given time and place for a given child. For example, a historical TV program on the Holocaust, the civil rights movement, or other major events, violence notwithstanding, may be a rich experience for a child coviewing with an interested parent.

Some video games and software also carry voluntary ratings for parents to use in deciding about the suitability of a product for a child. Both the Recreational Software Advisory Council and the Entertainment Software Rating Board developed ratings systems in response to legislation in 1994. However, studies have shown that only a minority of parents are aware of such ratings, even though most parents wanted products to be rated. Similarly, CDs and music cassette tapes may carry labels warning about explicit lyrics, once again as a cue for concerned parents. Some products also include the lyrics in narrative form. This is a mixed blessing; in the case of explicit or suggestive music lyrics, many young people are unaware of the meaning of these lyrics (or do not catch the lyrics at all)!

The National Institute on Media and the Family, a nonprofit organization in Minnesota, publishes trademarked, parent-friendly ratings called "KidScore" for children's media products on its website, including ratings for television series, movies, and video games. This system uses green (go), yellow (warning), and red (stop) symbols for parents, as well as explaining the content concerns. The National Institute on Media and the Family also publishes an annual "Video Game and Computer Game Report Card," including "The Parent Guide to Electronic Media," to assist parents in making optimal media choices for young people. . . .

Evaluating the Family's Media Use and Habits Regularly

Keeping a media diary or log helps families to assess media education progress. How many hours is our TV on each day? Are we making wise choices in our TV use? Our computer time? What kinds of programs have we enjoyed as a family? Since thinking about media time and media planning, have we changed our priorities as a family? Are we finding plenty of other pursuits to keep us engaged and challenged?

Parents and children can evaluate family discussions. Have certain TV programs or other media programs offered opportunities for critical thinking? Have any family members had a revelation about media images and messages? Are we better, smarter, more critical viewers now? It is important for families to continually self-examine the role media literacy plays in the family's everyday life.

> *"It is possible to reach the large firms that are the major advertisers and persuade them of the negative effects of sponsoring unwholesome programs."*

Advertisers Should Not Sponsor Violent Television Programs

Robert Stuart

In the following viewpoint, Robert Stuart, who served as CEO of Quaker Oats for fifteen years, argues that if major advertisers knew the consequences of sponsoring violent programs they could be persuaded to be more responsible about what shows they sponsor. According to Stuart, marketing executives make sponsoring decisions based on a program's profitability, not its quality. However, once CEOs realize that they are losing customers because their ads appear in violent shows, they might pressure their marketing executives to boycott such programs.

As you read, consider the following questions:
1. According to Stuart, why haven't advertisers done more about the negative effects of TV programming?
2. Why does the author believe companies should see the results of the Iowa State study?
3. What does Stuart think will happen if programmers and advertisers do not regulate their own businesses?

When I was the honcho of Quaker Oats from the late '60s through the '70s, we began to realize that television clearly was the best way to sell our products.

Some of us also began to recognize, and worry about, what effect TV programming has on behavior, particularly of children. Quaker Oats had Fisher-Price in those days, and we advertised a great deal to children. We tried to be good guys, adapting a code of conduct which wasn't enforced perfectly but set guidelines on what sort of programs we would and would not support. We tried to avoid being too goody-goody, but we were aware of the consequences of this very powerful medium.

Executives Too Busy to Watch TV

Why haven't more advertisers done something? For several reasons. First, most CEOs don't have time to watch much television. They count on their subordinates to check what's going on. If the CEOs do watch some television, they're probably watching a bit of sports, but most nights their briefcases are bulging or they're involved in social events. So the executives of the world are not concentrating on this issue.

Some, for example John Pepper of Procter & Gamble, will be better about this. Some are better organized than others. I never had time to watch much TV. But occasionally I would spot one of our commercials on a somewhat dubious program and I'd ask a marketing employee, "What are we doing on that show?" He'd say, "Well, Bob, you've only given me 5 million bucks for this product. The company is judging me and my bonus on the profitability of this brand, and the advertising agencies say that that show gives me the greatest reach for the money."

So codes are there in businesses, but it's tough to stick to them. Businessmen somewhat understandably say, "In a world of competition, we can't afford to unilaterally disarm."

Still, it's worrying how much has changed in the last 30 years since I started worrying about this issue. It's an example of what Senator Patrick Moynihan has called "defining deviancy down." The shocking footage in [the] video, "Wasteland" [which documents the graphic violence, sex and obscene language on television programming] would stir up anybody

The Cost of Controversy

Research by K.C. Montgomery and J. Cowan details how advertisers often recoil from being associated with controversial television programming. For a company, an advertisement on a prime-time network movie represents a significant investment. Reported advertising prices for a 30-second slot on prime-time movies in November 1995 ranged from $90,000 to $150,000 depending on the evening and network. To avoid sponsoring programs that may generate controversy for a particular product, firms often hire a company in New York (AIS) to prescreen prime-time network programs and alert them to content concerns, including violent and sexual content. Even without network warnings, major advertisers are thus apprised of the content of programs such as prime-time movies.

If firms find a program too controversial, they may pull their advertising from the show. Broadcasters may end up selling this advertising time at reduced rates or not selling it at all. The costs of controversy will vary by program and network. Robert Iger, president of Capital Cities/ABC, estimated that the network loses nearly $20 million in advertising revenues each year because of decisions by sponsors to avoid controversial programs.

James T. Hamilton, *Television Violence and Public Policy*, 1998.

concerned about our kids and the future of our society.

I think the time may have come when businessmen will do more. The new Forum for Responsible Advertisers is one sign of this, and one I support.

Looking at the Bottom Line

I think it is possible to reach the large firms that are the major advertisers and persuade them of the negative effects of sponsoring unwholesome programs. Companies should, for instance, be shown the important study done recently at Iowa State, backed by the American Psychological Association. It demonstrated that people actually become so irritated and annoyed by violence on television today that they can't remember the product that sponsored the show.

Businessmen are always thinking of the bottom line, and if we could get this point through their coconuts, that in sponsoring way-out stuff they're losing customers as well as doing social harm, then that's a significant economic force which may dissuade advertisers from blindly accepting any type of programming offered them.

There is much evidence that what people see on television can have serious adverse consequences. I think everybody would prefer to do something about the problem on a voluntary basis. But I'm convinced Congress is so upset about this that unless programmers and advertisers regulate their own house as businesspeople, and pull back from the really outrageous shows, then we're headed for the legislative regulation most of us don't want.

"Boycotting is a form of free speech. If it swept the country, movies might change."

Women Should Boycott Movies Showing Violence Against Women

Margaret Morganroth Gullette

Female viewers who repeatedly witness violence against women begin to feel weak and helpless, becoming vicarious victims, argues Margaret Morganroth Gullette in the following viewpoint. To combat the problem, Gullette claims, women must boycott movies that offend them and let men know that if they insist on seeing such depictions, they will go alone. Until movie labels accurately reflect what movies include such violence, maintains Gullette, people must warn each other about movies with violence against women. Gullette is a resident scholar in Women's Studies at Brandeis University.

As you read, consider the following questions:
1. What does Gullette claim are the goals of moviemakers?
2. In the author's opinion, what are the consequences for couples who see movie violence together?
3. How does the Hollywood rating system frame the media violence debate, according to Gullette?

Margaret Morganroth Gullette, "Reel Danger: Why Women Are Boycotting Movies," *On the Issues*, vol. 7, Fall 1998, pp. 12–13. Copyright © 1998 by On the Issues: Progressive Women's Quarterly. Reproduced by permission.

There is a quiet, subversive movement under way that involves women boycotting movies that depict violence against women. As I write this, I'm boycotting *Copycat* and *Breaking the Waves*; a film professor I know, *Nil by Mouth*; and two younger women, *Scream*. When I tell people I started my boycott after the stalking scene in *Silence of the Lambs*, women flare up with their own boycott histories. One named the Coke-bottle scene in *The Long Goodbye*. Another said disgustedly, "I walked out of *The Piano* right after he cut off her finger and the camera lingered on her lying in the mud." Everywhere I go—New England, L.A., Iowa; lunches, parties, weddings—I find these spontaneous little sects, relieved to have company in their resistance to misogyny. This is an unreported national movement, and making the boycott and its rationales known is all it needs to be effective.

We needn't agree on one another's choices. Rather, in these indignant groups, women focus on the dangers of adding to our already mountainous archives of sadistic imagery. We are full of ideas for improving the cultural climate.

The Problem of Vicarious Victimization

I was not becoming inured to violence by seeing more. Instead, like someone developing anaphylactic shock after consecutive bee stings, I was getting sicker. Every woman I know increasingly refuses to subject herself to the humiliation, sorrow, paranoia and terror.

My theory is that identifying with female victims can cause "vicarious victimization." This concept is all too familiar to domestic-violence counselors, who listen repeatedly to stories of threats, beatings, rape. They have learned that unless they too get counseling, they can become psychically weakened by continual exposure to such horrendous stories. To live even vicariously in a world structured by male violence against women is risky. Assailed by images of women unable to fight back or escape, counselors imagine themselves vulnerable and helpless.

All women are forced to live to some extent in such an imagined terrorist state. Battering, rape, and murder get reported ever more frequently by TV and newspapers, with horrifying details. Movies can do even more harm because of the emotive power of the narrative. Writer, director, cinematographer, editor, composer—all aim to heighten our sense of impending, appalling harm, to sharpen our dread. I fear this malice. I know the moviemakers had these goals in mind—not my pleasure.

Women who boycott instinctively understand vicarious victimization. They may reasonably fear that they will be weakened in their domestic relations with men. Merely deciding together on film fare may lead to arguments with one's partner. Sometimes his male pleasure in viewing eroticized violence treats her female "unpleasure" as a nuisance.

The Consequences for Couples

There are consequences for couples who see violence together. All intimate relationships involve constant negotiations, from sexual to psychological to parental and financial. A woman might find herself, after years of vicarious victimization, weakened in all these negotiations. One woman noticed that on the nights they see male-on-female violence, her partner regularly seems interested in having sex, although she's repelled. Is this still vicarious?

Warning men about becoming vicarious perpetrators is critical, especially in light of studies like that by Daniel G. Linz at the University of California at Santa Barbara, that involves college men watching violent and degrading images. The study showed that after such viewings, the men lost both their sense of repugnance at assaults and their empathy for female victims in real-life situations such as rape trials. Narratives of male-on-female violence help to normalize cruelty: Some men become less ashamed about escalating their power.

I connect desensitization both to arguments with one's partner and to actual battery and murder. So do other cultural critics. But they pull back from obvious conclusions. Todd Gitlin, New York University professor and author of numerous books on social criticism, wrote, "That media violence contributes to a climate in which violence is legitimate—and there can be no doubt of this—does not make it a significant contribution to violence on the street." I disagree. Using visual art to brutalize men and victimize women psy-

The Disempowering Effects of Media Violence

The results of the study "The Disempowering Effects of Media Violence Against Women on College Women" support the growing fears about the ill effects that may emanate from the media portrayal of violence against women. This is of particular concern in view of the fact that the vast majority of films flooding the video and movie circuit depict violence, and women's roles (if any) in these films are usually as victims. Further, it also raises questions about the films and other media depictions that are designed to arouse women's consciousness about misogynous violence. In portraying the violence against women, such films may disempower their viewers, which may serve to counter action rather than promote it. It is clear that future research is required to both confirm the results of this study, and to explore means by which media can be used to empower women and promote resistance against the prevalence of misogynous violence in society.

Penny Reid and Gillian Finchilescu, *Psychology of Women Quarterly*, 1995.

chologically is an evil. Boycotters resensitize us by saying, "This evil is urgent enough to cause women to protect themselves against it and to ask for men's cooperation."

Labeling Violence Against Women

The Hollywood rating system has failed us. The PG-13, R, X designations are essentially a form of age-graded titillation that doesn't address women's concerns, framing the debate as if it were about being "old enough" to endure violent images and "cool enough" to enjoy them. Some film reviews in newspapers and magazines now indicate negatives parenthetically ("violence"). But one word can't tell me what I would be letting myself in for. Reviewers need to get specific. They need a code with ample commentary. M for Murder. R for Rape. T for other Tortures. YBW when the victim is a Young Beautiful Woman, as she typically is. No fair talking up "esthetic values" without exposing a film's sexist inventions designed to elevate male testosterone and elicit good reviews.

Women get suckered into seeing movies they wouldn't have seen if they'd only known. I would have shunned *Death Becomes Her* if a reviewer had written: "T (Tortures). Female aging is so grotesque it amounts to mutilation." Despite its comic surface, the movie gave me nightmares. One comment on *Devil in a Blue Dress* should have been: "Red-hot poker prepared for . . . you guessed it, YBW." In the absence of sensitive reviewing, people warn one another. One woman said happily, "My sons warn me." If sons boycotted, the future could really be different.

One current effect of the boycott is that when men see movies labeled as desensitizing, they go alone. They leave at home their girlfriends, sisters, wives, and mothers. They sit by themselves. Eventually, some will realize—to borrow a phrase of one critic—"these are the stag parties of the damned."

Some kinds of film violence may be necessary. The scene of attempted rape in *Thelma & Louise* demonstrates bluntly how far women will go to protect each other. But the newest ploy is to justify violence as "empowering." In *Female Perversions*, not one but two actresses slice their own skin. Maybe people will stay away from that type of vicarious victimization in the same way that many African-Americans decide they don't need to see another movie with a lynching, no matter how well made.

Boycotters needn't be defensive. Being required to prove that we're not wimpy or Philistine is hostile. Let's turn the tables. Let's ask, "Why are YOU going?"

Need I say that all this has nothing do with censorship? Boycotting is a form of free speech. If it swept the country, movies might change. But if they do not, the human relations of the women who stay home—and the men who stay with them—would change profoundly. Nationwide recognition of boycotting would help to detoxify American culture and advance women's freedoms.

"Vigorous criticism of the perverse, hateful, and violent reflects a willingness on the part of citizens to take ideas seriously, evaluate them accordingly, and engage them directly."

The Public Should Criticize Violent Music Lyrics

Sam Brownback

Although the Constitution protects music that glorifies violence and debases women, Sam Brownback contends in the following viewpoint that people who find this music offensive must make their criticism public. A free society should not censor offensive music, Brownback argues, but free people must not be apathetic; a society that does not speak out against violent music sends a message that violence is acceptable. To uphold freedom and decency, American society must illustrate that it can judge between what is right and what is wrong by taking a stand against offensive music lyrics. Brownback is a U.S. senator from Kansas.

As you read, consider the following questions:
1. In what ways does music have a powerful public impact, according to Brownback?
2. According to the author, how are different people affected differently by music lyrics?
3. In Brownback's opinion, why is glorifying violence in popular music dangerous?

Sam Brownback, address to the City Club of Cleveland, Ohio, March 23, 1998.

I want to talk with you today about music and freedom, about lyrics, liberty and license. This is an issue that is important to me—as it is, I suspect, important to you. I can't think of a more fitting place for this discussion here, at a forum dedicated to upholding the principle of free speech, in Cleveland, Ohio, the home of the Rock and Roll Hall of Fame.

As many of you know, I held a Senate hearing on the impact of violent music lyrics on young people. During this hearing, we heard a variety of witnesses testify on the effects of music lyrics that glorified rape, sexual torture, violence and murder. Some of these lyrics are almost unbelievably awful but they are backed by huge, powerful, prestigious corporations. I have grown more and more concerned about the content and the impact of these lyrics. And I have publicly criticized the entertainment executives who produce, promote, and profit from such music.

When Opposing Music Is Not Censorship

I am also the only Senator on the Commerce Committee to vote against a very popular bill that would coerce TV stations into labeling their programs.

I publicly opposed V-chip legislation. I have consistently voted against any sort of government involvement in regulating or rating music or television.

Some people don't think the two go together. They think that if you talk about some music lyrics being degrading and violent, then you must be in favor of censorship. Others think that if you vote against various government restrictions on television programs, or music content, you must approve of those programs and songs. Both views are mistaken.

And today, I'd like to talk about legislating in a way to maximize freedom, and agitating for civility and decency, and why the two not only can go together, but should—and indeed, if we are to preserve freedom, they must.

The Power of Music

Most of you here have strong ideas about music. As indeed, you should. Music is powerful. It changes our mood, shapes our experience, affects our thoughts, alters our pulse, touches our lives. The rhythm, the beat, and the lyrics all impress us with their message. Thousands of years ago, the great philosopher Plato stated, "Musical training is a more potent instrument than any other, because rhythm and harmony find their way into the inward places of the soul, on which they mightily fasten."

When Criticism Is Censorship

Individuals have every right to speak out against music and films they find offensive. However, public criticism should not turn to calls for censorship or violence. The *Rocky Mountain News* published a letter to the editor April 22, 1999, which reads, "Marilyn Manson, along with all other purveyors of filth and violence, Hollywood in particular, should be indicted for murder, convicted and executed." In other words, shred the First Amendment and persecute people for their ideas and words.

While the comment is best interpreted as an isolated, emotionally charged outburst, it remains disquieting.

Ari Armstrong, *Independence Institute*, April 30, 1999.

As such, music lyrics have profound public consequences. In many ways, the music industry is more influential than anything that happens in Washington. After all, most people spend a lot more time listening to music than watching C-Span or reading the newspaper. They're more likely to recognize musicians than Supreme Court Justices. Most of us spend more time thinking about music than laws, bills, and policies. And that's probably a good thing.

And as many of you know, no one spends more time listening to music than young people. In fact, one recent study conducted by the Carnegie Foundation concluded that the average teenager listens to music around four hours a day. In contrast, less than an hour is spent on homework or reading, less than 20 minutes a day is spent talking with Mom, and less than five minutes is spent talking with Dad. If this is true, there are a lot of people who spend more time listening to shock-rock artist Marilyn Manson or Snoop Doggy Dogg than Mom or Dad. In fact, Marilyn Manson himself said: "Music is such a powerful medium now. The kids don't even know who the President is, but they know what's on

MTV. I think if anyone like Adolf Hitler or Benito Mussolini were alive now, they would have to be rock stars."

In short, because of the power of music, the time we spend listening to it, and the potency of its messages, music has a powerful public impact. It affects us, not only privately, but publicly. It helps shape our attitudes and assumptions, and thus, our decisions and behavior—all of which has a public dimension, and merits public debate.

Frankly, I believe there needs to be more public discourse over music. It is too important to ignore. Its influence reaches around the world. American rock and rap are popular exports. They are listened to by billions, in virtually every nation on earth. And for good or bad, our music shapes the way in which many people around the world view the U.S.—American music is the most pervasive (and loudest) ambassador we have. Unfortunately, its message is too often a destructive one.

Glorifying Violence Against Women

Over the past few years, I have grown concerned about the popularity of some lyrics—lyrics which glorify violence and debase women. Some recent best-selling albums have included graphic descriptions of murder, torture, and rape. Women are objectified, often in the most obscene and degrading ways. Songs such as Prodigy's single "Smack My Bitch Up" or "Don't Trust a Bitch" by the group "Mo Thugs" encourage animosity and even violence towards women. The alternative group Nine Inch Nails enjoyed both critical and commercial success with their song "Big Man with a Gun" which describes forcing a woman into oral sex and shooting her in the head at pointblank range.

Shock-rock bands such as "Marilyn Manson" or "Cannibal Corpse" go even further, with lyrics describing violence, rape, and torture. Consider just a few song titles by the group "Cannibal Corpse": "Orgasm by Torture" or "Stripped, Raped and Strangled." As their titles indicate, the lyrics to these songs celebrate hideous crimes against women.

Many of you may already know the kind of lyrics I am talking about. If not, it is useful to read some of them—they won't be hard to find; they are quite popular. Then ask yourself: what are the real-world effects of these lyrics? What do these lyrics celebrate, and what do they ridicule or denounce? What are the consequences of glorifying violence and glamorizing rape? Have record companies behaved responsibly when they produce music that debases women? You and your friends may come up with different answers. But they are good questions to think about. And I hope recording industry executives think about them as well.

It is a simple fact of human nature that what we hear and see, what we experience, affects our thoughts, our emotions, and our behavior. If it did not, commercials wouldn't exist, and anyone who ever spent a dollar on advertising would be a complete fool. But advertising is a multibillion dollar business because it works. It creates an appetite for things we don't need, it motivates us to buy things we may not have otherwise. What we see and hear changes how we act.

The Impact of Violent Music

Now think back to the music we have been talking about. How do these lyrics affect their fans? Different people will be affected different ways. Some teens are more vulnerable than others. Young people who grow up in strong families, going to good schools, with adults who are committed to them, are probably going to be just fine. But let's consider what happens in some of America's inner cities, where many young men grow up without fathers, without good schools, surrounded by violence—how does this affect the way they think about, and treat women? Moreover, there have already been several studies done that have pointed to a loss of self-esteem among girls and young women. How does the fact that some of the best-selling albums feature songs that refer to them exclusively as "those bitches and sluts" affect them?

There are no easy answers to those questions. It is impossible to quantify the ways in which such lyrics affect us. But it is equally impossible to believe they have no effect at all.

Of course, most rock and rap do not have hyperviolent or perverse lyrics. In the grand scale of things, it is a small number of songs from an even smaller number of bands that produce these sort of lyrics. They are the exception, not the rule.

It is also true that people will disagree over which music

is offensive. Some people thought the Beach Boys were a problem, and some think the Spice Girls are. I do not happen to be one of them. There will always be songs about which reasonable people with good judgement will disagree.

But there should also be some things that we can all agree upon. And one of those things is that music which glorifies rape, violence and bigotry is wrong. It may be constitutionally protected. The huge entertainment corporations that produce, promote and profit from this sort of record may have a right to do so. But it is not the right thing to do. . . .

For free societies to endure, there must be a distinction between what is allowed and what is honored. I believe that the First Amendment assures the widest possible latitude in allowing various forms of speech—including offensive, obnoxious speech. But the fact that certain forms of speech should be allowed does not mean that they should be honored, or given respectability. There are many forms of speech that should be thoroughly criticized, even as they are protected. Freedom of expression is not immunity from criticism.

Discouraging Those Who Promote Violence

The proper response to offensive speech is criticism—not censorship, and not apathy. Vigorous criticism of the perverse, hateful, and violent reflects a willingness on the part of citizens to take ideas seriously, evaluate them accordingly, and engage them directly. A cultural predisposition to care about ideas and to judge between them—while protecting the liberty of others, is the best bulwark of a free society. A citizenry that evaluates ideas, that discerns the true from the false, that values reason over reaction, that affirms that which is edifying, and that refutes that which is wrong—is exactly the society most likely to value, to have, and to keep free speech.

What we honor says as much about our national character as what we allow. There is an old saying "Tell me what you love, and I'll tell you who you are." The same can be said of societies, as well as individuals. What we honor and esteem as a people both reflects and affects our culture. We grow to resemble what we honor, we become less like what we disparage. What we choose to honor, then, forecasts our cultural condition.

This is important, because there are cultural conditions which make democracy possible, markets open, and societies free. Democracy cannot endure in a society that has lost respect for the law or an interest in self-government. Societies become less free when they become more violent. The more culturally chaotic we become, the more restrictions, laws and regulations are imposed to maintain order.

Glorifying violence in popular music is dangerous because a society that glorifies violence will grow more violent. Similarly, when we refuse to criticize music that debases women, we send the message that treating women as chattel is not something to be upset about. Record companies that promote violent music implicitly push the idea that more people should listen to, purchase, and enjoy the sounds of slaughter. When MTV named Marilyn Manson the "best new artist of the year" in 1997, they held Manson up as an example to be aspired to and emulated. Promoting violence as entertainment corrodes our nation from within.

This is not a new idea. Virtually all of the Founding Fathers agreed—even assumed—that nations rise and fall based on what they honor and what they discourage. Samuel Adams, an outspoken free speech advocate, said the following: "A general dissolution of principles and manners will more surely overthrow the liberties of America than the whole force of the common enemy."

Speaking Out Against Offensive Speech

Unfortunately, in many circles, liberty is being redefined as "license"—the idea that anything goes, that all speech is morally equivalent. According to this view, we cannot judge or criticize speech—no matter how offensive we may find it. After all, what is offensive to one person, the reasoning goes, may be acceptable, even enjoyable to someone else. Thus, the idea of honoring certain forms of speech and stigmatizing others becomes seen as infringements on liberty. This assumes that to have freedom of speech, you can't give a rip over what is said—and that tolerance is achieved by apathy. Their motto can be summed up in one word: "whatever."

This is dead wrong. A philosophy of "whatever" is poison to the body politic. Civility, decency, courtesy, compassion, and respect should not be matters of indifference to us. We should care about these things—care about them deeply. We should allow both honorable and offensive forms of speech. But just as certainly, we should honor that which is honorable, and criticize that which is not. If we, as a society, come to the place where we think anything goes, the first thing to go will be freedom.

The great southern author Walker Percy once stated that his greatest fear for our future was that of "seeing America, with all of its great strength and beauty and freedom . . . gradually subside into decay through default and be defeated . . . from within by weariness, boredom, cynicism, greed and in the end, helplessness before its great problems."

Determining Our Future

I am optimistic about our future, but his point is an important one. America is at a place in history where our great enemies have been defeated.

Communism—with all of its shackles on the human spirit— has fallen. The Cold War is over. Our economy is strong; our incomes up, our expectations high. We are, in a sense, the only remaining world superpower.

Certainly, the future looks bright. But our continued success is not a historical certainty. It will be determined by the character of our nation—by the condition of our culture as much as our economy, or our policies. What we value, and what we disparage, are good predictors of what we soon shall be.

This is why I have both legislated in a libertarian manner, and agitated against hateful, racist, violent music lyrics. For those of us who are concerned about the loss of civility in society, and the glorification of hate, violence and misogyny in popular music, our goal must be not to coerce, but to persuade. We should aim to change hearts and minds, rather than laws. Analyzing, evaluating, and sometimes criticizing lyrics is not only compatible with, but essential to, liberty.

May rock roll on, and freedom ring.

Periodical Bibliography

The following articles have been selected to supplement the diverse views presented in this chapter.

Sam Brownback   "The Melodies of Mayhem," *Policy Review*, November/December 1998.

Sam Brownback   "Needed: A Code of Conduct," *World & I*, April 2001.

Mary DesRosiers   "Rock Fans Fight Censorship," *Progressive*, June 1999.

Economist   "Hold That Tune," *Economist*, November 28, 1998.

Diwata Fonte   "Rapping the Music Industry's Knuckles," *Business Week Online*, July 26, 2001.

Susan Gutwill and   "Zero Tolerance or Media Literacy: A Critical
Nancy Caro Hollander   Psychoanalytic Perspective on Combating Violence Among Children," *Journal for the Psychoanalysis of Culture & Society*, Fall 2002.

Marjorie Hogan   "Media Education," *Pediatrics*, August 1999.
and Miriam Bar-on

Paul Klite   "Media Can Be Antibiotic for Violence," *Quill*, April 2000.

Jerry M. Landay   "Getting a Movement Moving," *Nation*, June 8, 1998.

John Leland   "Family's Patterns Can Blunt the Effect of Video Violence," *New York Times*, September 25, 2000.

Christina L'Homme   "Decoding Images," *UNESCO Sources*, June 1998.

Mike Mitka   "Watch What Kids Are Watching, Says AAP," *JAMA*, January 3, 2001.

Jesse Walker   "Bringing Art to Court," *Reason*, August/September 1999.

Bill Walsh   "To Know the Media Is to Rate the Media," *Billerica (MA) Minuteman*, June 7, 2000, www.medialit.org.

Tara Zahra   "Did Buffy Do It?" *Nation*, July 19, 1999.

For Further Discussion

Chapter 1

1. The Senate Committee on the Judiciary cites studies to support its claim that media violence leads to actual youth violence. Stuart Fischoff argues that many of these studies lack "external validity." Researchers, he claims, cannot generalize from the behaviors measured in the studies to predict real-world violence. What types of aggressive behaviors produced in the lab do you think would satisfy Fischoff that media and real-world violence were linked? Explain.

2. Stacy L. Smith and Edward Donnerstein claim that exposure to television violence is harmful. Jib Fowles questions this claim because he believes that people experience television violence in a different way than they do real-world violence. How does each author see the average television viewer, and how do these perceptions influence their respective arguments?

3. Dave Grossman argues that first-person shooter video games can transform children into unfeeling killers. Douglas Lowenstein claims that it is unreasonable to compare the shooting of animated characters to the killing of real human beings. How might each author's profession influence his position on the effect of video games? Explain.

4. Jib Fowles and Becky L. Tatum refer to a tradition of accusations against popular culture and corresponding attempts at censorship. They argue that efforts to establish causal links between the media and real-life violence constitute just another page in the history of assaults on new media and new cultural influences. Do you agree or do you think contemporary claims against the media are different from past claims? Explain.

Chapter 2

1. Joanne Cantor, Paul McMasters, Julie Hilden, and Dale Kunkel cite media violence research while constructing their arguments. Those who support government restrictions on media violence say the research proves media violence is harmful, particularly to children. Those concerned that government interference with the entertainment industry threatens free speech claim that the research does not prove media violence causes actual violence. Examine what each of the authors says about media violence research. After evaluating their conclusions about the studies, whose interpretation do you find most convincing? Why?

2. While Joanne Cantor and Dale Kunkel see violence ratings as a tool to help parents protect their children from violent content, Paul McMasters and Julie Hilden see ratings as a weapon that slashes the right of Americans to speak freely. Do you perceive violence ratings as a tool or a weapon? Why?

3. Danny Goldberg and Joe Lieberman disagree over whether the Media Marketing Accountability Act regulates the content of entertainment. Lieberman claims that the act allows the Federal Trade Commission (FTC) to intervene only when entertainment companies market products to children that the companies themselves rate unsuitable for children. Goldberg claims that because the act gives the FTC the power to determine what products entertainment companies can market, the act determines what movies, music, and video games will be released. Whose argument do you find more persuasive? Explain.

4. Paul Klite and Lawrence K. Grossman both agree that television news coverage of violent crime is excessive. Klite suggests that one solution is to require that news broadcasts have warning labels that alert the public to the harmful effects of violent content. Grossman claims, however, that government restriction of television news is unconstitutional, and instead he recommends public criticism. Which suggestion do you find most persuasive? Explain.

Chapter 3

1. Marjorie J. Hogan assumes that violent media will continue to enter the home and maintains that parents must therefore monitor their children's media habits. What obstacles do you think parents will face when trying to implement Hogan's suggestions?

2. Robert Stuart contends that businesses can respond to the problem of media violence by not sponsoring violent television programs. Do you think the entertainment industry would find Stuart's argument persuasive? Why or why not?

3. Margaret Morganroth Gullette and Sam Brownback each suggest different ways to express individual disapproval of entertainment that portrays violence against women. Gullette maintains that people should boycott movies that portray violence against women while Brownback contends that people should publicly criticize violent music lyrics, including those that debase women. Which method do you think would be more effective?

Organizations to Contact

The editors have compiled the following list of organizations concerned with the issues debated in this book. The descriptions are derived from materials provided by the organizations. All have publications or information available for interested readers. The list was compiled on the date of publication of the present volume; the information provided here may change. Be aware that many organizations take several weeks or longer to respond to inquiries, so allow as much time as possible.

American Civil Liberties Union (ACLU)
125 Broad St., 18th Floor, New York, NY 10004-2400
(212) 549-2500
e-mail: aclu@aclu.org • website: www.aclu.org
The ACLU champions the rights set forth in the Declaration of Independence and the Constitution. It opposes the censoring of any form of speech, including media depictions of violence. The ACLU publishes books, handbooks, project reports, pamphlets, and public policy reports. The ACLU website provides access to some of these publications as well as press releases, legal briefs and opinions, and legislative documents, including "Freedom of Expression in the Arts and Entertainment."

American Psychological Association (APA)
Office of Public Affairs
750 First St. NE, Washington, DC 20002-4242
(202) 336-5700
e-mail: public.affairs@apa.org • website: www.apa.org
This society of psychologists aims to "advance psychology as a science, as a profession, and as a means of promoting human welfare." Although the APA opposes censorship, it believes that viewing television violence can have potential dangers for children. On its website the APA provides access to its Adults & Children Together Against Violence program (www.actagainstviolence.com), which includes information on the impact of media violence and suggestions for parents and others who care for children, including the handout "Strategies to Reduce the Impact of Media Violence in Young Children's Lives."

Cato Institute
1000 Massachusetts Ave. NW, Washington, DC 20001
(202) 842-0200 • fax: (202) 842-3490
e-mail: cato@cato.org • website: www.cato.org

The institute is a libertarian public policy research foundation dedicated to promoting limited government, individual political liberty, and free-market economics. It publishes the bimonthly *Policy Report* and the periodic *Cato Journal*. Cato's website provides access to policy reports, congressional testimony, legal briefs, the current issue and archives of its quarterly, *Regulation*, and articles by Cato analysts, including "Rating Entertainment Ratings: How Well Are They Working for Parents, and What Can Be Done to Improve Them?"

Center for Successful Parenting
PO Box 179, 1508 E. 86th St., Indianapolis, IN 46240
e-mail: csp@onrampamerica.net • website: sosparents.org
Founded in 1998, the center was created to increase awareness of the negative effects of violent media on children and move the public to action to protect children from media violence. On its website, the center provides news, fact sheets, and tools to help parents protect their children from the risks of media violence, including the article "Can Violent Media Affect Reasoning and Logical Thinking?"

Federal Communications Commission (FCC)
1919 M St. NW, Washington, DC 20554
(888) CallFCC (225-5322) • (202) 418-0200 • fax: (202) 418-0232
e-mail: fccinfo@fcc.gov • website: www.fcc.gov
The FCC is an independent government agency responsible for regulating telecommunications. It develops and implements policy concerning interstate and international communications by radio, television, wire, satellite, and cable. The FCC is required to review the educational programming efforts of the networks. It publishes various reports, updates, and reviews that can be accessed online at their website.

Media Awareness Network (MNet)
1500 Merivale Rd., Third Floor, Ottawa, ON K2E6Z5 Canada
(800) 896-3342 • fax: (613) 224-1958
e-mail: info@media-awareness.ca
website: www.media-awareness.ca
The goal of MNet is to promote and support media education in Canadian schools, homes, and communities through an Internet site. The website encourages critical thinking about media information and stimulates public debate about the power of media, especially in the lives of children. MNet provides information for parents, educators, industry, and government. The media violence

page includes current news, legislation, and resources. A balanced variety of articles in media-violence debate can be accessed, including "Is Media Violence Free Speech? A Debate Between George Gerbner and Todd Gitlin" and "Prime-Time Violence."

Media Coalition
139 Fulton St., Suite 302, New York, NY 10038
(212) 587-4025 • fax: (212) 587-2436
e-mail: mediacoalition@mediacoalition.org
website: www.mediacoalition.org
The Media Coalition defends the First Amendment right to produce and sell books, magazines, recordings, videotapes, and video games. It defends the American public's right to have access to the broadest possible range of opinion and entertainment, including works considered offensive or harmful due to their violent or sexually explicit content. It opposes the government-mandated ratings system for television. On its website, the coalition provides legislative updates and access to reports, including *Shooting the Messenger: Why Censorship Won't Stop Violence*.

MediaWatch
PO Box 618, Santa Cruz, CA 95061-0618
(800) 631-6355
website: www.mediawatch.com
The goal of MediaWatch is to challenge racism, sexism, and violence in the media through education and action. MediaWatch does not believe in censorship but distributes educational videos, media literacy information, and newsletters to help create more informed consumers of the mass media and a more active citizenry. MediaWatch publishes articles, books, and videos, including *Don't Be a TV: Television Victim* and *Warning! The Media May Be Hazardous to Your Health*. On its website, MediaWatch provides current news and articles on media issues, including "Murder, Sex, Mayhem: Tonight at Six."

National Coalition Against Censorship (NCAC)
275 Seventh Ave., New York, NY 10001
(212) 807-6222 • fax: (212) 807-6245
e-mail: ncac@ncac.org • website: www.ncac.org
The NCAC is an alliance of national nonprofit organizations, including literary, artistic, religious, educational, professional, labor, and civil liberties groups. The coalition is united by a conviction that freedom of thought, inquiry, and expression must be defended. The NCAC works to educate members and the public at large

about the dangers of censorship and how to oppose them. Its website provides access to press releases, legal briefs, and congressional testimony on censorship issues including violence in the media.

Parents Television Council (PTC)
707 Wilshire Blvd., Los Angeles, CA 90017
(800) 882-6868 • fax: (213) 629-9254
e-mail: Editor@parentstv.org • website: www.parentstv.org
The goal of PTC is to bring America's demand for values-driven television programming to the entertainment industry. PTC produces an annual Family Guide to Prime Time Television that profiles every sitcom and drama on the major television networks and provides information on subject matter that is inappropriate for children. On its website, the PTC publishes movie reviews, television analysis: "Best and Worst of the Week," articles, press releases, and special reports, including the "Mature Video Game Family Hour Advertising Study."

Positive Entertainment Alternatives for Children Everywhere (PEACE)
2341 Duberger Ave., Suite 109, Québec City, PQ G1P 3N6
Canada
(418) 622-8383 • fax: (418) 622-3654
website: www.media-awareness.ca
The primary objective of PEACE, the English-language twin of Travail de Reflexion pour des Onde Pacifiques (TROP), is to raise awareness of the effects of media violence and press for changes in the media industries. PEACE sponsors an annual entertainment vote in school, in which students choose the most peaceful and the most violent television shows, video games, and music videos. PEACE shares the results with the community and communicates the results to government and industry leaders.

Rocky Mountain Media Watch
(303) 298-1426 • fax: (303) 292-9317
e-mail: info@bigmedia.org • website: www.bigmedia.org
Rocky Mountain Media Watch studies and documents the excess found in local television news across the country. It believes that programs are saturated with mayhem and fluff at the expense of the broader range of issues important to our communities. The organization claims that television news is currently designed to arouse viewers but does not inform citizens. Rather, it breeds cynicism, discourages civic participation, and promotes fearful withdrawal and passivity. Rocky Mountain Media Watch publishes

books including, *Not in the Public Interest: A Snapshot of Local TV News in America* and *An Honest Move from News to Entertainment.* The organization's website publishes articles, press releases, and downloads for media activists.

TV Turnoff Network (Formerly TV-Free America)
1601 Connecticut Ave. NW, Suite 303, Washington, DC 20009
(202) 518-5556 • fax: (202) 518-5560
e-mail: e-mail@tvturnoff.org • website: www.tvturnoff.org

TV Turnoff Network is a national nonprofit organization that encourages Americans to reduce the amount of television they watch in order to promote stronger families and communities. It sponsors the annual National TV-Turnoff Week, when more than 5 million people across the country go without television for seven days. On its website, it publishes news, articles, and the fact sheet "What Is TV-Turnoff Network."

UNESCO International Clearinghouse on Children, Youth and Media
Nordicom, Göteborg University
Box 713, SE 405 30 Göteborg, Sweden
e-mail: nordicom@nordicom.gu.se
website: www.nordicom.gu.se

The clearinghouse disseminates information about the relationship between young people and media violence, alternatives to media violence, and efforts to reduce violence in the media. It publishes a yearbook and *Influence of Media Violence: A Brief Research Summary.* On its website, UNESCO provides access to its database and current and past issues of its newsletter, *News on Children and Violence on the Screen.*

Bibliography of Books

Martin Barker and
Julian Petley, eds.
Ill Effects: The Media/Violence Debate. 2nd. ed.
New York: Routledge, 2001.

David Buckingham
*After the Death of Childhood: Growing Up in the
Age of Electronic Media.* Malden, MA: Blackwell,
2000.

Sandra L. Calvert,
Amy B. Jordan, and
Rodney R. Cocking
*Children in the Digital Age: Influences of Electronic
Media on Development.* Westport, CT: Praeger,
2002.

Joanne Cantor
*Mommy, I'm Scared: How TV and Movies Frighten
Children and What We Can Do to Protect Them.*
New York: Harcourt Brace, 1998.

Denis Duclos
*The Werewolf Complex: America's Fascination with
Violence.* New York: Berg, 1998.

Rose A. Dyson
Mind Abuse: Media Violence in an Information Age.
Montreal: Black Rose Books, 2000.

Kathleen J. Edgar
*Everything You Need to Know About Media Vio-
lence.* New York: Rosen, 1998.

Herbert N. Foerstel
*Banned in the Media: A Reference Guide to Censor-
ship in the Press, Motion Pictures, Broadcasting, and
the Internet.* Westport, CT: Greenwood, 1998.

Jonathan L. Freedman
*Media Violence and Its Effect on Aggression: Assess-
ing the Scientific Evidence.* Toronto: University of
Toronto Press, 2002.

Cynthia A. Freeland
*The Naked and the Undead: Evil and the Appeal of
Horror.* Boulder, CO: Westview Press, 2000.

Russell G. Geen and
Edward Donnerstein,
eds.
*Human Aggression: Theories, Research, and
Implications for Social Policy.* San Diego:
Academic Press, 1998.

Jeffrey H. Goldstein,
ed.
*Why We Watch: The Attractions of Violent
Entertainment.* New York: Oxford University
Press, 1998.

Dave Grossman and
Gloria DeGaetano
*Stop Teaching Our Kids to Kill: A Call to Action
Against TV, Movie, and Video Game Violence.* New
York: Random House, 1999.

James T. Hamilton
*Channeling Violence: The Economic Market for Vio-
lent Television Programming.* Princeton, NJ:
Princeton University Press, 1998.

James T. Hamilton,
ed.
Television Violence and Public Policy. Ann Arbor:
University of Michigan Press, 1998.

Sue Howard
Wired-up: Young People and the Electronic Media.
Bristol, PA: UCL Press, 1998.

Gerard Jones	*Killing Monsters: Why Children Need Fantasy, Super Heroes, and Make-Believe Violence.* New York: Basic Books, 2002.
Yahya R. Kamalipour and Kuldip R. Rampal	*Media, Sex, Violence, and Drugs in the Global Village.* Lanham, MD: Rowman & Littlefield, 2001.
Sonia Livingstone	*Young People and New Media: Childhood and the Changing Media Environment.* London: London School of Economics, 2002.
M. Carole Macklin and Les Carlson, eds.	*Advertising to Children: Concepts and Controversies.* Thousand Oaks, CA: Sage, 1999.
Norma Odom Pecora	*The Business of Children's Entertainment.* New York: Guilford, 1998.
W. James Potter	*On Media Violence.* Thousand Oaks, CA: Sage, 1999.
Monroe E. Price, ed.	*The V-Chip Debate: Content Filtering from Television to the Internet.* Mahwah, NJ: Erlbaum, 1998.
Daniel M. Shea, ed.	*Mass Politics: The Politics of Popular Culture.* New York: St. Martin's, 1999.
Dorothy G. Singer and Jerome L. Singer, eds.	*Handbook of Children and the Media.* Thousand Oaks, CA: Sage, 2001.
J. David Slocum	*Violence and American Cinema.* New York: Routledge, 2001.
Victor C. Strasburger and Barbara J. Wilson	*Children, Adolescents, and the Media.* Thousand Oaks, CA: Sage, 2002.
Ray Surette	*Media, Crime, and Criminal Justice: Images and Realities.* Belmont, CA: Wadsworth Publications, 1998.
Joseph Jay Tobin	*Good Guys Don't Wear Hats: Children's Talk About the Media.* New York: Teachers College Press, 2000.
UNESCO	*Children and Media Violence: Yearbook from the UNESCO International Clearinghouse on Children and Violence on the Screen.* Göteborg, Sweden: UNESCO, 1998.
David Allen Walsh	*Dr. Dave's Cyberhood: Making Media Choices That Create a Healthy Electronic Environment for Your Kids.* New York: Simon & Schuster, 2001.

Index